MW01275028

13

THE GINGER SERIES

how to sail
a boat

matt vance

AWA PRESS

First edition published in 2013 by Awa Press, Level Three, 11 Vivian Street, Wellington 6011, New Zealand.

ISBN 978-1-877551-85-7

ebook formats
epub 978-1-877551-86-4
mobi 978-1-877551-87-1

National Library of New Zealand Cataloguing-in-Publication Data
Vance, Matt.
How to sail a boat / Matt Vance.
(Ginger series ; 13)
1. Seafaring life—Psychological aspects. 2. Sailing—Psychological aspects. I. Title. II. Series: Ginger series (Wellington, N.Z.) ; 13.
910.45019—dc 23

Typesetting by Jill Livestre, Archetype
Printed by Midas Printing International Ltd, China
This book is typeset in Walbaum

Find more great books at awapress.com

Produced with the assistance of

ARTS COUNCIL OF NEW ZEALAND TOI AOTEAROA

To my family

MATT VANCE is a New Zealand writer who specialises in sailing stories from the South Pacific, the Southern Ocean and Antarctica. His articles and photographs have appeared in *New Zealand Listener*, *Boating New Zealand* and *Wilderness*. He has sailed and raced extensively throughout the Pacific and has an immodest enthusiasm for his family, an old yacht named *Siward*, and a motley collection of eccentric friends.

There is poetry of sailing
as old as the world.
ANTOINE DE SAINT-EXUPÉRY

Landfall

FROM THE SMALL CABIN of *Chance* I watch the towelling curtains that separate the cabin from the cockpit. Orange, red and yellow tropical fish swim in profile in a blue sea. As the boat rolls the curtain dances, giving the sensation of a real underwater scene.

The cabin is used more for storage than for sleeping: it contains old lifejackets, sails and rope that have become stiff with salt water. It is also where small children like me are stuffed when the sea cuts up rough on the homeward leg of a visit to our favourite island. Through a parting in the curtains I can see my father and his friend David easing the boat through the gusts; part nervous tension, part pure enjoyment is written on their faces.

This is my first memory of the sea and of sailing.

On land Dad and David were teachers, with all the trials of the classroom, the school board and parent-teacher evenings. Out at sea they were under the fleeting illusion of being free, beyond the reach of all that. Under sail, they were confronted with a simple set of rules that required them to observe intently, to engage their entire being in the enterprise of moving across the ocean.

Despite the enormity of their effort, Dad and his friend had little effect on the sea: I could see *Chance*'s wake being quickly zipped up behind, leaving no trace of our passing. The same could not be said of the sea's effect on the two men. I could see in their faces the sea subtly unzipping them, pulling out the stuffing that had been buried by life on the land, revealing things about the sailor that only the sea might know.

Chance's wake feathered white on a green sea, before dissolving into the general lopping swell that always accompanied a strong nor'easterly. The tension and exhilaration we felt on deck didn't seem to evaporate in the wake. If anything, these feelings were amplified as the swell rebounded around the hull of the boat. The laughs were louder and the lurches seemed scarier than anything on land.

In calm weather, children were allowed out beyond the curtain to roam the cockpit and help trim the sails. On special occasions I would be ushered on to my father's lap and allowed to steer. My small hands were barely able to grasp the varnished tiller, and Dad would have to use his weight to gently correct my erratic course.

Through the helm I could feel that *Chance* was alive as every puff of wind was converted into a quivering surge that rushed up my arms. In my father's lap I was insulated from responsibility: sailing was a game with a warm safety net as Dad reached out his strong hand and dumped power from the mainsail, or hauled the boat back from the violence of an involuntary gybe that had loomed, while I dreamed I might be that seagull over there. It was only when the sea got rough that, with urgent tones, we were corralled into *Chance*'s cabin. Pulling the towelling curtain across the hatch was a sign we were not to venture on deck and mess with the serious job of keeping the boat upright. There was no time for arguing or stalling or all the other stuff we might have tried on land.

While the other kids lolled around on the sail bags and had pillow fights with the spare lifejackets, I was always drawn to what lay beyond the curtains. The thought of what lay out there would give me a queer twisted feeling deep in my guts, accompanied by a dry furry mouth. This was part excitement, part outright fear. It is a feeling I still associate with doing things that make you feel really alive, things that have in them some possibility of catastrophe – and a good chance of something better than that.

This feeling was there on the first day I took the helm of my Optimist dinghy, *Tigger*. It was there for all of the 150 metres I sailed before pulling off a tack and returning to my father on the boat ramp. It was most definitely there when my friend's father said, 'She's all yours, boys' as he swung himself down into the companionway, slid the hatch shut and reclined on his bunk, leaving two nine-year-olds in control of a 40-foot trimaran on the open ocean. It was there when I took off down my first wave in *Tigger* – and at the bottom of the wave when I capsized spectacularly.

It was there on the night before a race when the wind howled in the trees around the house, and on the night before I departed for my first offshore voyage to Tonga.

From the stern of *Manaroa III* we watched New Zealand vanish. For most of the day it had been a faint smudge behind us, seeming to stick to the horizon until, after making a cup of tea below, I came up to the call of 'She's gone.' My stomach gave a churn that would become familiar. Departure from the land is a kind of death, and there was a reverent silence from the crew as New Zealand disappeared below the curvature of the Earth. There was nothing for it now. We turned, faced forward and took in the sea.

Among the crew of *Manaroa III* there was a peculiar mix of skills and talent, bound by the cement of humour and goodwill. Dave and Gwen were dairy farmers. Two years earlier they had sold a chunk of their farm to buy a bare steel hull of Denis Ganley design. Dave had proceeded to fit a tractor engine and weld the hatches closed. He had then issued earmuffs and a beanbag for comfort to each of the crew and motored 800 nautical miles down the coast to his farm, where the rusty hull was hauled out and deposited in his hayshed. Over time Dave and Gwen turned it into a work of art.

Having made our departure we quickly became a nation of five souls in a small speck of the Pacific Ocean. We had immediate concerns, such as changing sails and catching tuna to supplement one of Dave's bulls that had ended up in *Manaroa III's* freezer. Each evening the crew would crowd around the navigation table, listening to the warbling crackle of the single sideband radio presenting a collection of the only news that meant anything: the proximity of other boats and the developments in the weather. Chris, our navigator, would mark our position with a faint pencil cross on the chart. The gaps between marks, barely wider than his cigarette-stained finger, meant 24 hours of sailing. Such is the humbling vastness of the Pacific Ocean.

After a few finger widths across the chart we entered the beginnings of the south-east trade winds, the warm steady breezes that denote life in the tropical Pacific.

They meant days of beautiful downwind sailing, with fluffy clouds and squadrons of flying fish fanning out across deep purple water. At night we sailed in T-shirts as spectacular displays of stars wheeled above the mast, matched only by the spectacular displays of phosphorescence that spread out like galaxies in our wake. Day after day we reeled in the land that we hoped lay ahead.

One morning, after we had been eight days at sea, 'Ata, the southernmost of the Tongan islands, emerged out of the dawn. Since midnight *Manaroa III* had had a slight trip in her predictable trade-wind stride, the backwash of the swell thumping off the island, telling us of its presence ahead. This induced no dry mouth or queer feeling in the stomach. In fact it was the opposite: the sniff of a landfall roused the crew, who now came on deck bleary-eyed from sleep, clutching the edge of the cockpit like children let out from behind the towelling curtains.

By midday we were in the lee of the island, and despite it being uninhabited a strong smell of manure and sawdust and a hint of wood smoke wafted over the water to our deprived noses. For the first time in over a week *Manaroa III* sat upright, with only the faintest hint of movement. We rested in the lee of 'Ata for most of the afternoon, drunk in the pleasure of having conjured up land from the wide ocean.

Later we headed on to Tongatapu, Tonga's main island, and from there to the myriad beauty of the Ha'apais and

Vava'u to the north. When we finally went ashore we swayed with a bad dose of what Dave referred to as 'wobbly boots' and marvelled, like lunatics let out of the asylum, at the vividness of the tropical vegetation.

Our arrival was celebrated with a party that did not seem to stop. Dave and Gwen were delightful company and a steady stream of sailors and locals visited the boat. Once the guests were aboard Dave would turn to the crew and say with mock pomp, 'I think it is only fair and Christian-like to offer these folk a drink.' Poking my head up from the cabin one morning I counted two chickens strutting around the deck, three deckchairs, a plastic statue, and a banana palm, the results of a great night at a village feast.

Occasionally I would escape and head ashore to walk in the cool green bush. The Tongans I met on my wanderings would ask, 'Where's your family?' When I smiled and pointed south to New Zealand, they would dart concerned looks at each other about the palangi with no family and insist I visit their village, where I would be overfed and become an excellent source of entertainment for their grinning kids.

Eventually *Manaroa III* headed back to sea. We mourned the land as we watched it slowly vanish. From my bunk I could gaze through the sturdy companionway and watch Dave staring intently ahead. Behind him, the wake of the boat dissolved, leaving no trace of our passing.

*There are three sorts of
people: those who are
alive, those who are dead,
and those who are at sea.*

ANACHARSIS, sixth century BC

Sailors

THE BAY WHERE my yacht *Siward* is moored lies miles from the nearest marina. The bay has a pleasant aspect, an attractive swimming beach, and protection from the open ocean. It contains an assortment of cruising yachts, the odd fishing boat, and on a summer's day it has something wonderful you can't quite put your finger on.

It attracts a variety of modest, well-built boats. The sailors, like the boats, are unassuming and full of character, with a roundedness that all objects sloshed in salt water seem to take on over time. They make their livings as farmers, builders and wharfies, working with their hands. Like most people they have their dreams, but unlike the dreams of their landlubber friends theirs have names such as *Carly*, *Astra* and *Gypsy*.

The boats are double-ended, plumb-bowed, gaff-rigged, fractional-rigged: ketches, sloops, schooners, catamarans and keelers made of timber, steel, fibreglass and concrete. Some are immaculate works of art that show your reflection in their hulls; others are rough as guts, neglected, with guano-covered decks, and large forests of marine growth burgeoning from their under-water sections. The owners proudly defend their boats' attributes, as if the boats are their children and they are prepared to turn a blind eye to their eccentricities and errant behaviour.

Occasionally a new boat will turn up in the bay and the very look of it will lead me to unfounded conclusions, such as, 'He's definitely a Wharram catamaran sailor with socks, sandals, a beard and two girlfriends' or 'It's that bogan welder and his steel schooner with a chain-link steering wheel' – until I row over in the dinghy, get invited aboard for a cup of something, and discover they are a barefoot clergyman or a solo dad. When they ask if I would like my tea with sugar and then top it up with rum I know they will fit in just fine.

Very rarely is a second name used to describe these fellow boat owners. They are usually 'Jim from *Juneer*' or 'Rob from *Cabot*', as if their whole identity has been swallowed by the bay. It is at their funeral that you realise sailing has been only part of their life. Their other life, which is revealed in their eulogy, has a whiff of betrayal. I find myself saying things such as, 'Who would have guessed the old bugger was a devout Christian?', preferring the memory of a sailor with an immodest enthusiasm for gin and ribald jokes.

Occasionally a description such as Jim from *Juneer* is not enough. Some of the old fellows will look at you blankly and you have to resort to descriptions of the boat: 'You know, that beautiful steel cutter with the teak trim.'

'Oh yes – Jim,' they will say, the details of the boat being sufficient to cover everything from Jim's anatomy to his psychological makeup.

Like any collection of boats in the world, the ones in the bay are subject to the 90:10 rule. This is the quirk of human nature that means 90 percent of boats are rarely, if ever, sailed. Some are taken out of the water for servicing once every year or two, and spend the rest of the time sitting forlornly on their moorings. Others do not seem to have moved for years. They are surrounded by thick skirts of seaweed and look as if they may contain a dead body or two in their darkened cabins. These neglected dreams grow more decrepit by the year and take on the appearance of the sea itself. On calm nights they occasionally give up and sink at their moorings, or on stormy nights they cut themselves loose and commit suicide on the rocks. Dreams are hard to hold: they require inspiration, vision, and antifouling once a year to keep them afloat. Compounding this is fear, fear of actually getting out there and handling the boat, fear that the sea might find you out.

Among the ten percent of boats that do sail there are subspecies. Most notable are the boats of the tinkerers. The tinkerers don't enjoy sailing but enjoy boats. They keep their boats in immaculate condition. 'You could eat your dinner off that' is an expression you will often hear of their handiwork. They love getting lost in the detail of diesel engine installation and the labyrinth of electronic gadgetry that their boats seem to propagate. To step aboard and offer a simple, 'How's it going?' will elicit a detailed analysis of their compression test or the moisture content of the hull, which only more sugar in the tea will render interesting. As is their nature, tinkerers love to build boats and will spend a casual 20 years getting the details right. Getting the boat to the water is perhaps the greatest of life's disappointments for the tinkerer.

The sailors are a small minority, probably only half of the ten percent who are aboard their boats regularly. They are distinguished by their ability to handle their boats under sail and to have been over the horizon in them. Their boats are in working condition, well-loved and sailed, but you probably could not eat your dinner off them.

Morry from *Carly* is one of my closest neighbours in

the bay and he is a sailor. He has the kind of physique that comes from working the land for 40 years. He has a cheeky grin and never wears more than a pair of shorts and a flannel work-shirt, even in winter. I quite often borrow tools from Morry as he usually has six of whatever you are after and they are all sharp. *Carly* is an Alan Wright sloop and, like her owner, *Carly* is both capable and rugged. I often stop in at Morry's house as he has a good view of the bay and all the boats at their moorings from his lounge. When I am away from the bay I ring Morry to ask how *Siward* is faring. His standard reply is a deadpan, 'She's all good. I can just see the tip mast above the water at low tide.'

Morry's only two vices are chocolate and naps in his bunk at his favourite anchorage. For some of us it has become a tradition to quietly sail up to *Carly* when she is at anchor and loudly yell something like, 'Wake up, Morry, you terrible bastard.' As it is his habit to sleep with his head forward under the low foredeck, there is usually an audible clunk as his head hits the deck, followed by a string of sailorly oaths.

From Morry's lounge I watch Walter from *Trailblazer* rowing out in his dinghy. Walter is a warm-hearted Irishman with a well-founded Herreshoff sloop. He is a sociable fellow and enjoys fine company. I follow him through the binoculars, and without removing them from my eyes I wager, 'What's the bet he won't make his boat?'

'Extremely bloody likely, I reckon,' Morry says from the depths of his kitchen, where he is brewing tea and arranging chocolate biscuits.

We are referring to Walter's habit of stopping to talk, which sometimes consumes his whole afternoon to the point that he never reaches *Trailblazer*. To have Walter aboard for a chat is always an hour or four well spent.

Walter appears to have stopped at *Coriohan*, where a telltale trail of white smoke is coming from the chimney of the heating stove. *Coriohan* is a stunning North Sea gaff-rigged trawler built by Tommy, an Irishman who sailed to the bay from his homeland over 20 years ago. Tommy has bright sparkly eyes that hint he may have lived forever. He is married to a delightful Canadian named Lynn, who is always happy to see you and, like most Canadians, has an aversion to the cold. She stokes the wood fire such that if Morry is aboard when you arrive he will say, well out of Lynn's striking range, 'Welcome to the SS *Sauna*.'

Beyond *Coriohan* there is the unmistakable outline of Stu from *Rhapsody* rowing out to his Athol Burns cutter. Stu's stroke is strong and military-like, which fits with his job as an SAS soldier. When Stu is on leave he is always on *Rhapsody*. When he is not, he disappears for three months at a time to places such as Afghanistan and Iraq. Stu has the physique of someone who could kill with his bare hands and sometimes this attribute replaces his boat's name in his description, so that it becomes 'You know, Stu of the kill-you-with-his-bare-hands'. Luckily for all of us, Stu is a great sailor and a nice guy.

With my eyes still in the binoculars, I notice a white launch that is only sometimes in the bay. 'I see the sleeper is back,' I say to Morry, who is now beside me at the window, slowly sipping his cup of tea. 'Yes, a mysterious bugger indeed,' Morry says, before chomping into his chocolate macaroon.

The sleeper turns up two or three times a year and picks up his mooring. He is obviously no sailor as he approaches the mooring downwind, relying on horsepower to stop him. He then proceeds to lock himself in the cabin and pull all the curtains. He is never seen on deck and remains in this state for up to three days before disappearing again. We have all secretly speculated on the sleeper – who he might be, and what thoughts cross his mind in the darkened cabin.

Each year the Mooring Association sends me its bill. I always shuffle it ahead of all the other bills and pay it promptly. For the princely sum of one hundred dollars I get a mooring inspection and an invitation to what is considered the social event of the year, the annual Mooring Association barbecue.

Morry is part of the three-strong barge team that pulls and inspects the moorings each year. With a hint of *Last of the Summer Wine*, the three gentlemen of the barge appear to be having great fun as they hand-crank the mooring chains to the surface. If you row past them while they are engaged in their toil you hear such comments as, 'Who was the ham-fisted bastard who did up this shackle?'

I look forward to the Mooring Association barbecue. Even if it occurs on a good sailing day it is worth missing out on a sail to catch up with some of the finest folk around. I am the youngest there by about a hundred years and am roughly the age of most of their children, who now live somewhere else that does not have bellbirds or sea breezes. Some of the old fellows keep a mooring for their children in the vain hope they will one day come home to the bay. Chances are they won't, so some of this attention reflects on to me.

The barbecue takes place at the rugby clubrooms above the bay and it is the usual community affair: cremated sausages backed up with BYO salad. The topics of conversation are kept broad, welcoming and full of good humour. I regale our table with impressions of Walter almost falling off his perch as he comes alongside the wharf in *Trailblazer* while the local female sun-loving contingent is indulging in a nude swim. 'You'll catch your death of cold dressed like that, young girlie,' I say in a mock Irish accent. There is a snort of laughter as Maureen tries to contain a mouth full of beer.

Most of the people at the barbecue are sailors, with just the odd tinkerer among them. Stu, back from some war-torn corner of the Earth, and Jim from *Juneer* are discussing the sleeper. Their eyes turn as a couple walks in. The man is wearing white pants and the woman a sailor's felt cap. Both items arouse my suspicion, and when the pair come and sit at our table my suspicion is confirmed: they have joined the Mooring Association without mooring or boat.

John is harmless enough, full of bluster and boasts that belie the fact he can't sail. His wife, Shirley, is harder to accommodate. Cloaked in heavy makeup and jewellery and looking like a cape pigeon with a startled expression, she has clearly come to the conclusion we are a bunch of hicks. Eventually she sucks all the oxygen out of the conversation at our table, and then, during a natural pause in the room's talk, declares over the top of her chardonnay, 'Of course we wouldn't keep our boat here. The cruising in Marlborough Sounds is far superior.'

There ensues an awful silence. All these sailors who are their boats politely nod and stare at their glasses of warming beer and secretly wonder whether Stu's hands are twitching.

A sailor's joys are as
simple as a child's.
BERNARD MOITESSIER

How to really sail a boat

THERE IS A GOOD reason that Awa Press did not print this book on waterproof paper. If you are now aboard and quickly leafing through these pages to find out how to tack your boat, you are in trouble. Take the honourable way out: toss the book over the side and follow it smartly, leaving the crew to it. This will be far less painful than trying to learn boat handling from a book.

There are plenty of folk who have tried to learn using this method. If you are curious about the result read John Caldwell's book *Desperate Voyage*. It will cure you of attempting such a monstrous thing.

In the words of science writer David Quammen: You have not asked for advice so I will now give it. In fact, advice is the first storm you will have to weather on your journey to becoming a sailor. There is no shortage of stuff out there on how to sail a boat. However, not all advice is equal, and learning how to get the good stuff will be your first test.

You are probably smart enough not to ask advice from landlubbers. These people constitute a fair portion of the population and, while some are harmless enough, keep in mind that landlubber logic has brought us talk-back radio, nuclear weapons and line dancing, all good reasons to completely disregard their ideas.

There is a dangerous mob that lies somewhere between the sailor and the landlubber. This comprises landlubbers masquerading as sailors. Do not, under any circumstances, take advice from them. They are easy to spot as they will call themselves sailors, talk loudly in the bar, and offer unsolicited advice at the mere hint of the sea in a conversation. They may wear white pants, boat shoes and sailors' caps, but underneath this nonsense they are landlubbers and will dish out lubberly advice. When they open their mouth to talk, the sensible option is to place your fingers in your ears and scream until they go away.

Good sailors are harder to spot, and only sailors will be able to identify a good one for you. This reeks of a secret society but is nothing as sinister as that, just large doses of humility dished out by the sea. A good sailor will speed up your learning process and save you from some of the more avoidable disasters that await. Not all sailors will have the patience to teach you, which is even more reason to ask around to find the ones that can. Take your time as good advice is worth it.

Part of looking for a good sailor and good advice is finding someone who will take you on a trial sail. This trial sail will be a good check to see if your dream matches reality before you commit yourself to becoming a sailor. If sailing is your thing this will be the easiest way to find out, and if sailing is not your thing you will be able to confidently ignore the white sails heading down the harbour on a summer's morning and not have your heart sail with them.

Once you have tracked down your good sailor, make sure it *is* they who take you for your first sail. Avoid all offers from well-meaning uncles or white-pant poseurs – they will only frighten the sailor out of you with their incompetence.

A good sailor will choose a nice sea breeze for your first experience and will talk you through what is going to happen. They will answer your questions and correct your mistakes gently and with good humour. If they like you they will offer you the helm. Take it and your face will not be able to hide the simultaneous fear and wonder of feeling something living surge up your arm. The good sailor will smile at this. Give a little bit. Offer to do jobs around the boat and help put it to bed after the sail. If your good sailor shows any reluctance to take you sailing, go for a bare-faced bribe. Good rum will do it, but not the cheap stuff. Even if they don't show reluctance, douse them with rum.

Sailing a boat, like many other things in life, is all about anticipation. This can mean anticipating the weather next week, or reading the next gust that darkens the water to windward. Anticipation is what makes sailing look easy and at its core is observation. After a time you will be able to spot sailors in meetings: their eyes will wander beyond the conversation to the window, where they will be watching clouds, and signs of wind in trees.

Learning to observe the wind and the sea will take some time. Ask your good sailor what they see when they look at the sea. Pay attention to the weather and develop an unnatural fixation with the barometer. Study birds, smoke and treetops and how they react to the wind. Most importantly, watch other sailors intently.

Up until now you have had your hand held. Now you want it on the helm of your own boat. As the sniper loves the trigger, this desire will possess you. Some of you may even skip the hand-holding bit in your haste to gain possession of the helm. This is a harder road, yet it leads to the same place.

You will get your helm but keep in mind three things: on your first sail do not inflict your combination of passion and incompetence on anyone else – any punishment should be yours alone; be prepared to fail repeatedly to get your techniques right; and be prepared to swear a lot.

Those points have probably eliminated most of the readership, so for the few of you left here is the next step. If you are dead set on taking the helm, find yourself a dinghy to sail. A dinghy will teach you boat handling, which is the fundamental literacy of being a sailor. While buying a 40-foot keeler and sailing an errant course over the horizon has been done before, it will hand out hard and expensive lessons. A small sailing dinghy will dish out punishment for bad decisions swiftly, often and cheaply, which is exactly what you need to whip the landlubber out of you and beat boat handling into you.

The boat will have to be able to be capsized and hauled upright again without fuss or the retention of vast volumes of the ocean. Something like a Laser Radial – or a Starling, if you are of smaller stature – is fine. You can buy one cheaply, or borrow one from a good dinghy sailing club. Choose a warm summer's day with a light sea breeze. Ask a good sailor to help you rig the boat and get you into the water.

Your first voyage out and back will loom large in front of you. There may be a twisty, gripey feeling in your guts. This will be fear, and the only way to relieve it will be to capsize the boat and learn to right her. That's going to mean getting in the water, so wear a life vest and dress accordingly. Spend as long at this as it takes to get confident that capsizing is not the end of the world. After a while you will get so good at it you will be able to capsize the boat and stay dry. Keep working on this until the fear subsides.

With the worst-case scenario dealt with, you can now focus on the sailing. Reaching will be the easiest point of sail to learn on – that's with the wind 90 degrees to the boat. You will no doubt be accustomed to the wheel steering of the automobile, so steering by tiller will take some getting used to. The basics of sail trim can also be learnt on a reach. Ease it out until the front edge, or luff, of the sail lifts. You will also have to keep the boat upright by concentrating your weight on the windward side and shifting it in and out to balance the boat.

While you have been experimenting with sail trim and steering, you will be heading towards an inevitable point at which you will have to turn the boat around and head back. First time up, you are best to turn the boat into the wind. This is called a tack and it will mean two things: you will have to change sides or the boat will fall over, and you will need speed to get the boat to steer where you want.

This is no time to be timid. Get the boat's speed up, push through the tack, shift your weight to the other side, duck under the boom and head back where you came from. All this will go through your mind as you stall the boat, backwind the sail, get caught on the leeward side, and capsize the boat. Keep trying until you get it. Swear lots.

You will eventually make it back to where you started, and if you are bold you will do this exercise again and again for a whole afternoon. That first journey there and back will loom like Everest in your life and you will never forget it. You went somewhere and came back, using only your wits and your strength to harness the most wonderful form of free energy on the planet.

Much later you will learn the violence of the gybe, the balance of the helm, and the fine trimming of your sail. You will learn the value of repetition, so that everything about the boat becomes second nature to you. You will be able to sail her upwind and downwind, sail her without a rudder, sail her backwards, and feel her get up and plane down a wave in a strong breeze. You will learn how to control the power of the sail and lift from your centreboard. You will begin to sail with your head up and out of the boat, anticipating the gusts and the waves. You will learn it all again when you start to race and are forced to make decisions and manoeuvres caused by things other than the elements.

You will learn to sail with a crew and you will learn to sail at night. You will learn to tell yarns about hairy experiences and characters you have met. You will be pushed until there is nothing left but your ragged little soul and you will experience the privilege of the trade winds, phosphorescence, and the green flash at sunset. You will learn how to control your fear and take responsibility for others. You will learn seamanship.

Then one day a wide-eyed landlubber will sidle up to you and ask you to teach them to sail. Another sailor will have recommended you. You will select a nice sea breeze to take them for a sail in your boat. You will answer their questions and correct their mistakes gently and with good humour. If you like them you will offer them the helm. Their face will show both fear and the wonder of feeling something living surge up their arm. You will smile. After the sail they will offer you rum, good rum.

*There are only two colours
to paint a boat, black or
white, and only a fool would
paint a boat black.*

NATHANAEL HERRESHOFF

The boat

THE AMERICAN AUTHOR E. B. White wrote in an essay entitled 'The Sea and the Wind that Blows': 'If a man must be obsessed by something, I suppose a boat is as good as anything, perhaps a bit better than most. A small sailing craft is not only beautiful, it is seductive and full of strange promise and the hint of trouble.'

Like White, who is best known for his much-loved children's book *Charlotte's Web*, I dream about boats constantly. It's been a lifelong affliction. Some people would tell you that what White called 'voyaging into unreality driven by imaginary breezes' is not a good thing. These people will most likely be landlubbers or registered medical practitioners. What they don't know is that a boat is as near to the physical representation of a dream as is possible on this Earth.

My dreaming of boats is like a film that is spooled and ready to roll at any available moment, flooding my thoughts as I wait for a bus or wander away from a less than compelling conversation. My favourite time to think about boats is during meetings. When I'm asked to contribute I have to be careful not to blurt out 'Lee-oh' or 'She's dragging' in case I get taken the wrong way.

When I was 12 I used to think I was the only one who dreamed like this until I attended a slide show at my local yacht club. Graham Donaldson, a young New Zealander, had sailed his beautiful sloop *Siward* 15,000 nautical miles from London. I sat transfixed in the front row as he spoke my dreams out loud. Far from being a theorist, Donaldson had the practical skills to turn his dreams into reality – he was a living example of what T. E. Lawrence called 'a dreamer of the day'. In that dim room I came to the realisation it was okay to fill my mind with visions of boats, and that dreams can have curvaceous hulls, slender rigs, and that air of strange promise.

A close ally of dreaming of boats is watching them. Any chance I get I find my way down to a harbour. Once there, I try on each boat in my head to see how it fits; I look at every nuance of rig and hull to see what the sea might see. It is acceptable to stare at other people's boats and praise them. If you did the same thing on land with houses, it would be called stalking and viewed dimly in the eyes of the law, but in a sailor's world it is a compliment, and will likely lead to a long conversation as the boat's owner recognises a kindred spirit.

For a while I would drive through Ōamaru each week on my way south. I would buy lunch at the tea rooms and then walk down to the quaint harbour to indulge in a little boat watching. After casting my eyes over the odd collection of craft, I would linger on a white-hulled sloop. There was something familiar about her.

It is said that a boat will find you good friends, nearly kill you at least twice, and save you from the curse of being financially wealthy. It is usually the last bit that people worry about. Like life itself, owning a boat is far more exciting if it rests on a firm foundation of financial insecurity. In reality you can spend as much or as little as you want on a boat, provided you are not afraid to sail her. Bernard Moitessier, a French yachtsman and author of five books on sailing, once said, 'She will cost you as much as you have', and that is as near to the truth as we can get.

Boats, like people, come in all shapes and sizes and have all manner of personalities, hang-ups and psychoses. The trick is to find one that matches your own quirks. Sail as many different kinds as you can and take note of how they make you feel. A good racing boat should scare you a little and make you want to call for Mum. A good cruising boat should make you feel you never want to go ashore again and that you could perhaps sail forever. Other boats are just plain fun: they are about the joy of getting wet and hollering your lungs out.

With the dream of boats goes the ownership of boats. Ownership is when the fantasy meets the hard laws of physics and, like the application of bat to ball, it can produce some spectacular results. What you are looking for is a boat that brings out your best bits while tolerating your weaknesses. As a kid I needed a boat that gave me confidence – I was intimidated by the sea and everything else. I inherited a black P-class called *Streak*. She was a vicious pig of a boat, naval architecture at its worst. The combination of a bad boat, my lack of weight, and a summer of strong nor'westers very nearly knocked the sailor out of me. Knowing when to drop a boat and keep searching is the key. You will need to own a few before you get it right.

Sometimes the dreams of the sailor do not make it to the sea. Boats have a physical presence and are hard to move. They can be found rusting in the backyards of any town you care to name; vivid orange streaks stain the ground around them when it rains. Even in this form they make good places to sit and dream and, for a young boy scared of everything, a good place to imagine sailing the world. For others, they are an uncomfortable reminder of who they could have been had they followed the visions of their youth.

The sea is what gives a boat her personality and draws the song from her. This song will be felt most strongly through her helm, and to hear it you will have to sail her. The helm, be it tiller, wheel or foot, is the window to a boat's soul. If she is a good boat you will know it through the helm and may count yourself a lucky sailor.

Nearly anything will float, but beauty in the eyes of the sea, closely followed by the eyes of the owner, is what will matter in the end. To be beautiful in the eyes of the sea a boat must have practical things, such as solid construction, ease of handling, and a balanced rig. In the eyes of the sailor, she must have all this plus a beauty that makes your spirit soar at the sight of her. To look at a beautiful boat is to instantly see yourself at her helm in a sea breeze on an endless summer afternoon. Of all the complex elements that make up a yacht, beauty is the one that should never be compromised. As Nathanael Herreshoff, the godfather of yacht design, said, 'There is no excuse for sailing an ugly boat.'

Love for a boat can be expressed in many ways. South African sailor Frank Wightman was prone to hugging the mast of his beloved *Wylo* after long absences. An observant dockside loafer in the Caribbean who witnessed one of these embraces called across the water, 'Do you want'a be alone whit her, captain?' Love can also take the form of alternate neglect and tenderness. My good friend Nick from *Windflower* ignored his beautiful sloop for three years. After finally hauling her out of the water he handed out beers to his drunken volunteers, who stripped two-metre lengths of seaweed from her underside with garden hoes procured from an elderly neighbour. It's a hard job to hoe a boat and when one of the volunteers dug too far and chipped her paint, Nick rushed to her defence like a gallant knight.

Just occasionally you may find a boat that is the love of your life. It will have many things, but most of all it will have an indefinable beauty. The first time I had seen *Siward* was when Graham Donaldson sailed her into my home port. Years later, as her unmistakable lines shone at me from Ōamaru's sleepy little harbour, I finally worked out why she was so familiar.

I asked around and tracked down her current owner. 'No,' Arch answered when I asked if she might be for sale. He was a fastidious, chain-smoking accountant who had bought her from Donaldson and kept her in mint condition. Over the next year I would visit him whenever I passed through town. 'No' remained the answer in what was turning out to be a kind of courtship. With each 'no' I would drive down to the harbour and watch her gently nodding at her mooring. Arch was very much a tinkerer and we were in the awkward position of having eyes for the same girl. Despite this, I was growing to like the old bugger.

As I slowly wore him down, he granted me privileges. I was able to visit *Siward* on her mooring. She had a wonderfully predictable motion and the smell of well-oiled timber was sweet in her cabin. These visits only strengthened my resolve. Arch would fend me off with lines such as, 'She's a lot of work, you know, an old wooden boat like this.' He figured I was an errant youth who would just bash her round and neglect her. Convincing him otherwise was taking time.

As part of Arch's crumbling resolve I was granted a test sail. *Siward* already had beauty in my eyes so it was beauty in the eyes of the sea I was looking for. Beyond all the cosmetics of hull colour and upholstery she was the kind of boat built with the sea in mind. The conditions were testing, a squally nor'wester and a lumpy leftover sea from the south. Arch was uncomfortable and smoked the whole afternoon while I grinned at the helm. I asked again as we rowed ashore. The answer was still no.

One early summer's day I called Arch to ask him yet again. To my surprise there was an uncharacteristic pause, followed by an unconvincing, 'Yes.' I shot down to Ōamaru that evening. It is said that the happiest time for a sailor is when they are buying or selling a boat, but fussing over his fastidious paperwork Arch did not look happy. His cigarette trembled in his hand. He was selling a little of his soul and I was buying some of mine back. *Siward* was no longer an ephemeral dream; she was real and full of strange promise. I rowed out to her that night and lay in the port bunk listening to the sounds the water made on her iroko planks and the gentle hum of her rig in the wind.

All loose things seem to
drift down to the sea,
and so did I.
LOUIS L'AMOUR

I see the sea

I AM IN FRANCE building boats. How this has happened is a minor mystery. Perhaps I have been attracted to the place because the French love sailing almost as much as New Zealanders do. And then, once I arrived, I was destined to become a boat builder for no other reason than that the Irish skipper of a 65-foot ketch called *Talina* did not like the French and preferred to employ Antipodeans.

I spend long days in the yard, where the air is filled with the whine of electric sanders and the low banter of boat-builders' French. Every evening after work I peel off my dusty overalls and go down to watch the sea. By the time I escape, the heat of the day is radiating off every surface.

It has become a necessary pleasure, the shedding of my skin and the short walk from the boat-builders' yard to the shimmering waters of the Bay of Biscay. Along the way I note which brand of beer the derelicts are drinking, an indication it's on special at the supermarket on the corner.

I nip in and buy my obligatory icy cold can. It chills my hand as I walk the remaining distance to the sea wall. 'I see the sea and the sea sees me' repeats softly in my head. The words recall an old childhood game my sister and I used to play in the back seat of the family car on the way to our favourite bay. So insistent is its message that my lips move involuntarily to the beautiful rhythm of the lines. The anticipation of seeing the sea is as strong now as it was then. Perhaps more so than for my sister, it has soaked into my soul.

My pace begins to slow as I gain the sea. From a low concrete wall I take in the unfolding vista. Speech and thought seem to desert me as I dedicate myself to watching, observing and seeing the sea. There is a wafting south-westerly breeze ruffling the water, which is twelve kinds of blue. The tide is on the ebb, leaving signs of the paths it has dug in the sand. Out beyond the beach a white sail is hard on the wind.

It is a summer's evening and there are plenty of people promenading along the sea wall. Most see the

sea as a stage set, a static background against which
they act out their lives. Occasionally, while deep in
discussion of their woes with their friends, they will toss
it a glance.

Among this throng I have noticed there is one other
sea-gazer like me. I can tell by the way he is standing, as
if in a trance, and by the way he looks at the sea. He is
a Frenchman to the core, his teeth clamped on a
cigarette and on his feet the trademarks of a fellow boat
builder, old trainers covered with epoxy resin. We nod a
greeting: the language barrier is too great to strike up a
conversation. There is a faint smile as he notices I have
the same brand of derelicts' special beer in my hand as
he does. Our eyes turn quickly back to the sea and all that
it is telling us.

Good sailors are natural sea-gazers. At a glance they
can take in the wind and its effect on the ocean and get
an indication of what the immediate future may hold.
Bad sailors do not gaze; like the promenaders along the
sea wall, they see the sea as a static thing to skip across
without getting their feet wet.

From the outside it may look as if the sea-gazer is
depressed. On more than one occasion I have been asked,
'Are you all right, dear?' by a kind old woman out walking her dog. On the inside, though, it is quite the opposite:
the gazer is experiencing warm reassurance that the sea
is going about its business, oblivious to the workings of
humankind.

Even before seeing the sea, a good sea-gazer will have noticed the wind. For the most part the wind will set the character of the sea, which in turn will set the behaviour of the boat. At its essence, wind is Earth's way of distributing heat. In hot areas, the air rises and causes low pressure. In cool areas, the air descends and causes high pressure. Wind is a perpetual attempt to equalise the two systems and in doing so it keeps our climate and planet habitable. On land the influence of wind is mostly ignored, yet when wind blows over the sea it becomes the sculptor of waves and the engine of currents. It brings the ocean to life.

Victorian poet Algernon Swinburne wrote of watching the 'wind's feet shine along the sea'. While not a sailor, Swinburne was most definitely a sea-gazer of the first order. When wind moves over the surface of the sea it has an instant effect on the motion of the water and its ability to reflect light. For a sailor, reading the effect of wind on water is a fundamental literacy. It illuminates the near future for those whose movement and safety is based entirely on the wind.

To a person of the land this may seem like sorcery. On more than one occasion I have been confronted with the statement 'But you can't see wind!' I refer them to Swinburne and point to the subtle colour changes of the wind's footprint on the water and the way the changes are broadcast through the helm of a boat. On the shores of the Bay of Biscay my fellow watcher makes no such bold allegations; he merely sips his beer and observes the sea in companionable silence.

Sea-gazing, like all good addictions, has its degrees of affliction. Maurie, my crewmate on an icebreaker that traversed the Southern Ocean between New Zealand and Antarctica a lifetime ago, was, if anything, worse than me.

I enjoyed sea-gazing from the low aft deck of the ship, a place others had named Copacabana Beach on account of the odd wave that broke there. This gave the place a sense of danger, of being right on the water among the towering swells of the wildest ocean on earth. Maurie preferred to do his sea-gazing from high above the bridge, where he recorded it all on video.

Late at night, when the lights on the ship's deck blotted out the world around us, I would join Maurie below decks in the lecture room and he would play his video of the sea. We would discuss the mysteries of the ocean while the room pitched and yawed to the rhythms of the west swell as it echoed on the large flickering screen.

Sailors and sea-gazers are naturally obsessed by weather forecasts: they are the marine equivalent of tarot card readings. Modern satellite technology has greatly improved the technical side of this dark art. However, old-fashioned sky-gazing still has its place. Maurie and I were often on the bridge of the icebreaker for the one o'clock weather fax. We had the shameless enthusiasm of junkies waiting for their next fix. In between the tight-packed lines of barometric pressure we would foresee monstrous storms approaching. Others on the bridge learned to watch us intently as we pored over the weather charts, and would ask us questions such as 'Will it be rough at dinner?'

The sky above the Bay of Biscay is foretelling a blow. Way up high there are wispy mares' tails in the clouds, and these are confirmed by the latest weather charts and a dropping barometer. The Frenchman has no doubt noticed all this. Like me, he knows we will soon experience one of the notorious gales that fill the bay with their rage.

There is the faintest hint of a groundswell licking along the edge of one of the offshore islands. This has made landfall during the day from somewhere deep in the North Atlantic, and judging by its size it has travelled a long way. The first outrider of the approaching storm, it is gradually beginning to dominate the normal low roll generated by the local sea breeze. At any one time there are several different swell patterns and directions on the open sea. The shorter they are the closer they have formed; the longer they are the more distance they have travelled. This effect alone gives the sea a vitality that no lake can touch. To look at the open sea in this way is, like star-gazing, to look at the past, present and future, all in one take.

By now the last dregs of my beer are warm. The drink has rinsed the gritty taste of sanding dust from my mouth and the sea has filled my lungs with its salty breath and dulled the whine of electric sanders from my ears. I raise my eyebrows in a goodbye to the Frenchman and amble off home for my dinner, like a child reluctantly leaving a playground.

By next afternoon the gale is upon us. This is a nor'wester and its violence suggests a prisoner destroying his cage. From down in the hull of *Talina* there is a haunting din of wind in the rigging. The boat is now a musical instrument, with taut strings of wire plucked by the wind and amplified into the curved sound box of the hull. At its most benign the boat's music may be a lullaby, but today it is a chorus of demonic moans.

The filmmaker's adage 'The pictures tell you what is happening and the soundtrack tells you how to feel' most definitely applies to boats. All day I listen to the eerie music emanating from the rigging; each time it climbs a note I feel an involuntary clenching somewhere deep inside.

The wind has also got under the skin of the other boat builders in the yard: they have retreated into the cafeteria and are consuming more wine than normal at their afternoon happy hour.

A quick 'À bientôt' and I am off, battling my way down to the sea. As I zigzag through the grid of streets I am alternately leaning into the wind and being frogmarched by it. Even the derelicts have been spooked by the sea's fury and are nowhere to be seen.

Well before reaching the sea wall I can hear the ocean's deep booming roar. Its tranquil blue has been transformed into fiercely foaming brown. I lean on the wall and into the wind. 'I see the sea and the sea sees me' is torn from my mouth. For the first time in a while I do not have to whisper the words: there is no chance of anyone hearing them. There are no promenaders. I am in sea-gazers' heaven and the only one mad enough to be out here.

From the corner of a watery eye I spot a figure struggling against the wind along the sea wall. The Frenchman stops nearby and removes a can of beer from his pocket, the supermarket special. As he opens it and toasts me the wind blows the froth clean out of the can. We grin at each other and then turn our eyes back to the spectacle of the sea. We watch for hours.

Health, south wind,
books, old trees, a boat,
a friend.
RALPH WALDO EMERSON

A most dangerous book

I T'S THE KIND OF BOOK I give people and say, 'Just read it.' I own three copies and at least two are usually out on loan. I found the original in a musty second-hand bookstore. For the sum of $9.95 I held in my hands the sailor's dream, lived out in 252 glorious pages and 25 black and white plates.

Sailors sometimes fasten themselves to rare books. *South Sea Vagabonds* is just such a book. It was published in October of 1939, well before advertising campaigns were the fashion, and written by a man who was not a writer. The book was too quirky to be an instant bestseller, but slowly over time the power of its simple narrative worked its way on board the boats and into the hearts of sailors throughout the world.

The book's author was a 29-year-old New Zealander named Johnny Wray, former accounts clerk, amateur boat-builder, sailor and dreamer. Although Johnny was an avid reader he had never published anything until he wrote *South Sea Vagabonds*, nor for that matter did he publish anything afterwards. *South Sea Vagabonds* was the singular work of a lifetime.

In the preface there is a stark personal statement: 'I am not a writer. Never was, never will be. I remember distinctly that my form master at school used to describe my attempts at essays as "conglomerations of facts occasioned by heterogeneous concatenations of stupid irrelevancies". And I don't know if I have improved much since then.' This is as close as Johnny gets to bullshitting us. The rest of the book is too good not to be true.

Johnny was splendidly out of step with his time. When *South Sea Vagabonds* was published, dropping out and cruising the South Pacific would not have been seen as acceptable in a world priming itself for a second great war. After the war, however, society was ripe for change. Long-range cruising began to gain popularity: it was no longer the realm of a few courageous souls like Johnny. Among these sailors and dreamers, Johnny's book found a following. They discovered it not with marketing hype and midnight sales but from wide-eyed friends who thrust it into their hands and whispered with missionary zeal, 'Just read it.'

I keep a copy of the book on my boat. Every year or so I get it down from its shelf, slide into my bunk and go with Johnny aboard his cutter, *Ngataki*, as he brings her to life with scrounged materials and ingenious economy. His writing style has you convinced you are a member of the *Ngataki* club, celebrating the triumphs of launching and laughing through the disasters with the sureness that only shared adversity and a sense of community can bring.

His story is sketched out in bare sentences, parched chapter headings and dry humour. The bringing about of Johnny's dream of sailing the oceans required the start of the Great Depression and his getting the sack. He had £8.10 in cash, a clapped-out motorbike and time on his hands. With the odds stacked firmly against him, he set about designing and building his dream ship.

In the sailor's world there are those who tinker and those who sail. Johnny was not a fastidious tinkerer but a sailor embarked on a boat-building project far beyond his capability. Compounding the problem, he had to scavenge most of the tools and materials. In the two years it took to build his boat, Johnny learnt some valuable lessons: kauri needs a lot of steaming to bend without splitting; unsupported frames will topple and knock you out cold; a Royal Enfield motorcycle will carry a 44-foot mast and a half-tonne engine scavenged from a turnip field; and it is possible to get 24 tonnes of boat and truck across a six-tonne bridge.

Ngataki was brought to life in a rough tin shed that Johnny knocked up next to his parents' house. He cannibalised the mains power from the house in such a fashion that the shed became live in wet weather 'so that it became a matter of some doubt as to what parts you could touch without getting a shock'. The tin shed became a virtual drop-in centre for the errant youth of Auckland. Johnny's friends formed the *Ngataki* club. The subscription was the sale of a book of raffle tickets and a contribution to the weekly keg that was drunk in the emerging lines of *Ngataki*.

When presented with the conundrum of how to fasten the kauri planks to the frames of *Ngataki*, Johnny came up with an unconventional solution — he would fasten them with fencing wire. He confesses, deadpan, that 'there was another small factor that had something to do with my adopting this method. I had no small bolts, whereas my father had a large coil of fencing wire he did not want'. To protect the steel wire from rusting Johnny scraped up bitumen from the road and hot-dipped the wire in it before baking the wire in his mother's oven while she was out.

A carvel-planked boat such as *Ngataki* is an unusual concept in that it is a series of timber planks held apart (not together) by cotton caulking. The well-proven theory of the time was that the cotton expands on contact with water, swelling to fill the gaps between planks and sealing the entire hull. Caulking cotton, by virtue of its important job, has to be of the finest quality. With limited funds Johnny's supply of good quality caulking cotton did not do the entire hull. Without as much as a blink he tore up the best quality cotton he could find: a few pairs of his pyjamas, three shirts and the odd vest.

By a warm summer's day in 1933 Johnny had finished his boat: he was about to cross the barrier from tinkerer to sailor. For many this is a transition never made, as evidenced by the peculiar New Zealand phenomenon of boats squandering their lives away on back lawns.

The launching of *Ngataki* was nothing short of spectacular. Getting her from the tin shed to the road proved the most harrowing ordeal. The skids that were laid down were inadvertently overgreased and 'travelling at a giddy pace, she reached the end of the long length of skids and, with a shuddering, thundering crash, she nose-dived and skewed around. Her bow ploughed deep into the asphalt and then went through a stone wall at the side of the path.' She was dropped again as she was jacked on to the trailer.

This would be enough to finish most modern yachts, but the *Ngataki* took it in her stride, in no small way due to her stout construction. The *Ngataki* club members were out in full force, with the usual keg or two of beer to lubricate proceedings. The party was well underway as the boat floated off her trailer for the first time, only faltering briefly as she began taking on water: the opening for the propeller shaft was unsealed. Another keg of beer was procured and the cork bung used to plug the leak while the party went on.

The effort required to build a boat can sometimes leave the builder in a state of paralysis once the craft is launched. The building has left them spent and the sailing of the boat is too scary to contemplate. Johnny overcame this with his usual enthusiasm and collection of renegade friends. He set out as soon as he could and learnt all he needed to on the water. Some of the lessons, such as being caught in a cyclone in the Tasman Sea and rolled 360 degrees, were tough. Others, such as getting *Ngataki* to self-steer in trade winds and discovering which of the seven suns that appeared in the old damaged sextant was the correct one, were easy.

Never short of an idea, Johnny attempted to become a trader. He sailed to remote Sunday Island – today's Raoul Island – and collected swags of a delicious variety of orange that grew wild there, with the intention of selling the fruit back in Auckland. However, things did not quite go to plan. 'We had quite a good cruise, interesting and instructive; but you could not say it had been a roaring success from a financial point of view. For, with a cheerful disregard of economics, the crew had eaten all the profits.'

South Sea Vagabonds is not just about building and sailing a boat, it is about a passion for simplicity and making do. It tells us life is incomplete without dreams and risk. It teaches important truths that are hard to appreciate in a life on land: oceans are beautiful and violent; friends are precious; and there is a use for a ferret on a boat. It's about how to dream and how we might live.

As the book ends Johnny is contentedly living his dream in Tonga. In the soft trade winds and turquoise waters of these islands he has written his book. He has married Loti, the love of his life, and now has the powerful combination of a good wife and a good ship.

First published in 1939, *South Sea Vagabonds* would appear in eight languages and four editions. To buy it now you will have to search hard in musty second-hand bookstores, pay a bomb online, or have a good person press a copy into your hand with a wide-eyed stare and the words, 'Just read it.'

In 1943, with the Second World War raging, Johnny sold *Ngataki* and joined the Royal New Zealand Air Force as a flight sergeant. He spent the war years at Mechanics Bay and Hobsonville with the flying boat fleet before the Air Force worked out he was colourblind. As soon as he was discharged he built *Waihape*, a stout 43-foot motorsailor, and moved to Waiheke Island, where he assumed the noble title of fisherman.

Ngataki passed through several owners. In the spirit of Johnny, these owners invariably attempted alterations with economy in mind, using scavenged materials and robust construction. The boat was inherited by Debbie Lewis and in the early 1990s completed a seven-year circumnavigation of the globe under her care, a remarkable feat for a 63-year-old yacht made of driftwood, fastened with fencing wire, and caulked with pyjamas.

It was Debbie who made the final decision to donate *Ngataki* to Tino Rawa Trust, a body set up to help preserve historically important New Zealand vessels. The trust moved the boat to a tilt-slab shed in Helensville and lovingly restored her to her former rough glory. She is now moored in Auckland's Viaduct Basin, where her beamy lines are admired in the hushed tones of reverence usually reserved for cathedrals.

As for Johnny, it wasn't electrocution from a live shed, falling overboard, or being crushed by a boat falling from its cradle that saw him on his way. It was simply cancer. His end would have made a good final chapter in his book: no sentimentality, only a good yarn. He died in 1986, but more importantly he died on his boat, *Waihape*.

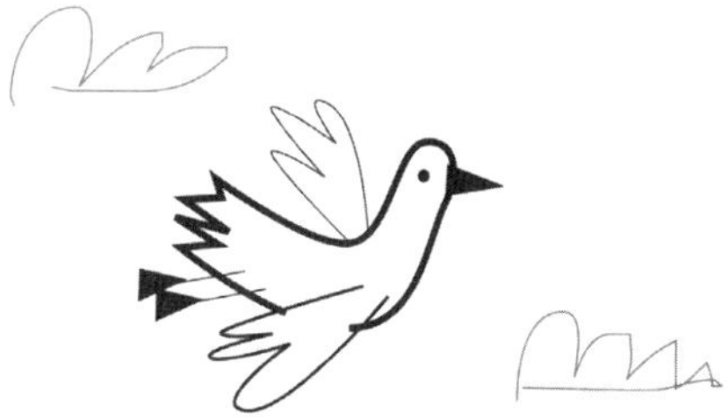

Any damn fool can
navigate the world sober.
It takes a really good sailor
to do it drunk.

FRANCIS CHICHESTER

The rat effect

HAD WE BEEN SAILING a cruising yacht we would have slowed down. We were not. We were sailing a stripped-out racer, and were in the throes of a race from Wellington to Gisborne. The relentless quest for speed drove us on through the pyramid-shaped seas, rendering a motion not unlike being in a car crash every 15 seconds. Tucked down in the dim cabin we were stacked like sardines in three tiers of bunks, keeping our weight where it was needed on the windward side.

From the deck came the call for yet another change of sail. Baldric and I slithered out of our bunks and fought our way into our wet-weather gear. As we slid open the hatch to feed out the No. 3 jib one of the periodic larger waves hit, sluicing green water over the deck and down the hatch, bowling Baldric and me off our feet, and filling our gear with sea water. We ended up facing each other in a pool of bilge water, sail bags and rope.

The shock left me speechless for a moment. Then my sleeping bag floated by. 'Bugger this, Baldric,' I sputtered. 'I reckon I'm a cruising man.'

This race was memorable for other reasons too, like the after-match party at which the crew were audacious enough to steal a faux Venetian statue from a local hotel and return it before anyone noticed. However, it was my awakening among the squalor and bilge water that I remember most. It defined the point at which the comfort of a nice anchorage, good company and a comfortable bunk overrode the need for speed. It defined the point where I began to appreciate the magic of cruising under sail, something I had known all along but not fully acknowledged until my sleeping bag floated by.

Cruising under sail is the equivalent of taking the long way home. It is the art of relaxing, enjoying the sail and savouring the idea of a destination. While the drama may not be as intense as that of racing, this is made up for by the richness of experience that cruising offers. Speed is not the god to which all comfort is sacrificed. In fact it is the lack of speed that allows the cruising sailor to relish the surroundings.

As a general rule, cruisers and racers do not mix. The racer cannot tolerate going slow, just as the cruiser cannot understand pushing a boat until she breaks. They peer at each other over what is one of the great philosophical divides of sailing.

Part of the art of cruising is selecting the right people to go slow with. Even the most extravagant cruising yacht will have cabin space equal to that of the average suburban bathroom, and for most it is less than that. No matter how well you think you know someone or get on with them on land, this can put a blowtorch on your relationship. Unless the team has been welded by shared adversity or revelation, there is potential for personalities to grate in sensational fashion. On the racing boat, on the other hand, all effort is put into making the boat go faster and making the team work better. This sense of sacrifice seems to override any expectations of comfort and any minor personality clashes.

Jim from *Kororo* had a habit of signing on old climbing friends for his annual cruise north. When I asked him why he had a crew who did not know one end of a boat from the other, he simply replied, 'Climbers love misery.' It was a fair call: without doubt it is the nature of the people, not their sailing skills, that is the most important asset of a cruising crew. The basics of helming and trimming can be taught in a short time. Not so the art of being good company.

Arthur Beiser said of the cruising boat's crew: 'Four people, if they are the right ones, are better when something ambitious is in prospect, but six may be crowding things. With more than six the rat effect takes over: past a certain critical density, rats in a cage go berserk.'

Beiser, a professor of physics at Harvard University, spent his summers cruising the coast of Maine in his 57-foot ketch *Minot's Light*. His book *The Sailor's World* delightfully captures the 'why' of sailing. It is part practical manual and part work of poetry. Arthur was in love with sailing and in love with his boat but among all this romanticism was his academic passion: theorising. The rat effect was the most famous of his theories and revealed his acute observation of the social habits of the sailor in motion.

The closest I have come to experiencing this syndrome was on a large cruising yacht in Pelorus Sound. During the day we fished and sailed and got on famously with each other, but the night rendered something akin to a bad zombie movie. The three bachelors of the crew, including me, were confined to the single men's quarters in the forepeak. Upon going to bed there would be a silent half-hour before Chris would start talking in his sleep. Chris's shore trade was carpentry and for most of the night we endured voluminous one-sided conversations with sub-contractors, clients, and even his bank manager. Not to be outdone, my other cabin mate, who had a habit of sleepwalking, would be out of bed and clawing at the hatch with a less audible but more rambling diatribe.

There have been volumes written on what constitutes a proper cruising yacht. Indeed Arthur Beiser produced a book entitled exactly this. He agreed entirely with the famous American naval architect Nathanael Herreshoff, who stated that for a yacht nothing short of 40 feet long was acceptable. This sort of theory is best left to the extremely wealthy. The fact is that for cruising nearly any boat will do. The more agile, simple and easy-to-sail a boat is, the more likely it is to be sailed. The bigger the boat the less likely it is to be sailed; size seems to give a yacht a sort of inertia, fuelled partly by intimidation and partly by inconvenience, which holds her to her moorings. Ideally a boat should be able to be sailed by one person. Others coming along should be a bonus: you can choose the sanity of solitude, or shipmates with whom you are willing to share your kingdom.

The right boat can eventually be found by trial and error. However, severing the bonds that hold the sailor to the shore is not so easy. There are the bills to pay, and the birthday parties and corporate barbecues to attend. Left unchecked, these can smother a sailor and slowly render them a landlubber. Part of this is that people of the shore are convinced the sailor will be subverted by the freedom of the sea. They are right of course, which is even more reason to slip the moorings.

Cruising usually implies a destination or a quiet anchorage. Islands and bays are always high up on the list, as is any piece of geography inaccessible by land. Inaccessibility alone seems to give these places a magical quality: when you approach them from the sea it is as if the boat has dreamed them into existence.

Occasionally there is no such destination to aim for and cruising for cruising's sake becomes the objective. The little coastal town in which I grew up had only the wide South Pacific and the monotonous sweep of a grey shingle beach. On Sundays the cruising fleet would sneak out early in the morning and begin beating to windward in the sea breeze. Feeling the pulse of the long ocean swell and seeing the land shrink into a long thin sliver was exciting beyond measure for a small boy. Around three in the afternoon each yacht would tack, set a spinnaker, and run home. The timing was never mentioned, but with the hindsight of adulthood it is clear it was carefully calculated so the sailors would be home in time for the opening of the club's bar – in itself a noble destination.

Arthur Beiser offered other theories around the vices of the cruising sailor. 'A man accustomed to a drink or three at lunchtime will not be pleased when the skipper locks up the bottle until nightfall.' He followed this up with the boldest of his assertions: 'Seldom will two women get along if this is their first time in close quarters.'

I quoted these from the hatchway of *Siward* to my friend Dan, who was taking a trick at the helm as we cruised the northern bays of the local peninsula. 'Not sure about the last one, but the first one might have some merit,' Dan said, eyeing the rum bottle stored away above my bunk.

Dan is notable for his ability to attract the unhinged and for doing a superb rendition of 'The Old Grey Mare'. Both are admirable attributes to have in a good crew. On this occasion, in addition to the right crew, we had the perfect number of people aboard. More than two and *Siward*'s limited accommodation and small cockpit become overcrowded.

It was a pleasure to escape the land and narrow our concerns down to 27 feet nine inches of boat. We took turns at the helm, regaling each other with half-baked theories such as the rat effect while spotting dolphins and penguins lolling around between dives. Denis Glover described these bays as 'the inlets of blind promise' and as we passed each one I suggested a potential anchorage.

'She wants to keep sailing,' Dan said. He was right. *Siward* was leaving a hissing wake, her rig humming with approval. It seemed almost criminal to break the spell.

The sun was getting low when we came abeam of one of the bigger bays on the peninsula. 'Looks like this is the one she wants to spend the night in,' Dan said. Up to this stage our yarns had been long-winded, but as we made our way up the bay they began to take on the rhythm of our short tacks. Each time we tacked the rattle of sails and sheets was like the time-up buzzer, curtailing our stories and signalling a change of topic and speaker.

We glided in on the last of the breeze and picked up a mooring for the night. It was very rare to see another boat in these waters so it was with interest that we noted a white-hulled sloop anchored on the other side of the bay.

I was busy cleaning up the confusion of sails and ropes on the foredeck when Dan piped up, 'She's coming over.' Sure enough, the sloop was close by. She had a healthy air of neglect, as did her helmsman, who introduced himself as Godfrey and promptly tied up astern of us. We were invited aboard for a quick tour and could see that Godfrey's cheerful manner had clearly been helped along by the best part of a dozen spent beer cans rolling around the cabin floor.

When we all retired to *Siward*'s small cabin, Godfrey drank three beers to our one, and devoured Dan's gourmet cooking. The sun was well down by now and the stars of Southern Cross hung above the hills of the bay. Conversation naturally turned to boats. Godfrey liked the nitty-gritty detail. He ventured to ask if we knew anything about the Jordan series sea drogue, a device for slowing down a yacht in storm conditions to prevent it pitchpoling end-for-end in big seas. As we spoke *Siward*'s anchor chain rumbled across the bottom like the closing of a rusty cage.

Not far into the discussion *Siward*'s guests began to argue as only New Zealand farmers (or perhaps fishwives) can, each holding their ground and not giving an inch; sentences began with 'You can't tell me' or 'I find it hard to believe.' Godfrey's arguments had the circular quality of someone well in their cups. Fuelled by Dan's well-placed verbal jabs, they began to spin even faster. My attempts to change the topic were quickly rebuffed and I was relegated to the role of spectator.

After a long half-hour everything came to an abrupt stop as Godfrey got to his feet. Turning to me, he swayed slightly and slurred, 'I appear to have offended your friend.' He reached for the rum bottle that lay on the chart table, took a long gurgling draft, then placed the bottle down carefully while wiping his mouth with his sleeve. 'Good evening, gentlemen,' he garbled over his shoulder, as he staggered up through the hatchway and disappeared into the night.

Dan stared blankly out of the hatch. *Siward*'s backstay hummed in the light northerly breeze. The rat effect had taken hold.

The chance of mistakes
is about equal to the
number of crew squared.
TED TURNER

The green
room

O F YACHT RACING, Arthur
Beiser said, 'One plated ashtray
and you are hooked for life.' He
was referring to the addiction of
speed and position, and the desire to take big risks and
endure moist privations in return for well-worn clichés
and tacky trophies.

'There'd better be at least a meatpack spot prize at the
end of all this,' rumbles our bowman, Jason. I doubt he
has read Arthur Beiser, but he has come to the same
conclusion after yet another energy-sapping sail change.

We are perched on the windward rail of a 40-foot
Davidson racing yacht called *Archon*, punching our way

south down the Sydney coast and bound for Hobart, with 352 other yachts bent on getting there ahead of us.

Life as bowman on an offshore racing yacht is a wet job. Already Jason's eyes are red from being fire-hosed by the bow wave, and the constant ingress of water has rendered his wet-weather gear useless. I had toyed with the idea of hosing down the interior of the boat prior to departure to short-circuit the demoralising influence of everything slowly getting soaked. I share my idea with Jason and he grins approvingly.

On my other side in the huddle on the windward rail sits Phil. Phil has been a driving force on shore and a large part of the reason we got to the start line in the first place. He would not let anything get in the way of his dreams, not even a gammy leg or lack of finance. He was going to do this race if it killed him.

He has been silent for a while. I ask if he is okay. 'Yep, wouldn't be dead for quids,' he wheezes, before throwing up his breakfast, some of which must have landed on the crew down the rail, judging by the cursing coming from that direction. Phil wipes his mouth and flashes me a weak grin before hunkering down to a solid four days of hell.

Racing is the natural by-product of another boat appearing on the horizon. It has its roots in naval warfare, and the primeval instinct that makes one mob think they are better than the other mob. Even the most laid-back of cruising sailors will begin tweaking the sails and darting looks over their shoulder should another boat appear nearby.

Racing means the boat will be pushed to its limits and the crew will have pressure applied, rendering small moves and big thoughts critical. This pressure will bring to the surface something psychologists call the core personality, unfettered by civility and with a dagger clenched firmly in its jaw.

On board *Archon* we are blessed with a collection of sailors able to channel their dagger-clenching personalities into the shared goal of making the boat go fast. We are blessedly free of scone-doers, screaming egos, and hindsight geniuses. The crew's only vices are swearing like sailors and having the potential to drink too much at the after-race party. You could trust your life to them.

By the second day, as we near the beginnings of Bass Strait, the initial headwind has swung to a quickly building tailwind. The strait is notorious because its shallowness buckles harmless swells into grey-bearded monsters and its narrowness seems to compress and accelerate the wind. As usual during the off watch there has been no sleep, only food and a little rest from the elements. Down below we have heard the telltale music of a rising breeze – the mounting roar of the bow wave and the twangs of a loaded rig.

When it is time for our watch on deck we struggle into our wet-weather gear and casually listen to the tail end of the weather report crackling over the radio in the navigation station. The news sounds grim. Jason slides a rough hand over his tired face and mumbles, 'Shit, this is going to get interesting.' I hand out muesli bars and we stuff them in our pockets. Without saying it, we all know they will have to last us for the next few days.

Going on deck is always a shock to an off-watch crew. The sensation is similar to jumping out of a plane. One by one we slither up into the cockpit in between waves of white water sweeping over the deck. Behind the helmsman the seas are beginning to stand up, turning pale green as the sun shines through them.

Phil crawls past on his way to the hatch and the relative luxury of a wet bed and a bucket. He is gaunt from seasickness. He pats me on the shoulder with a weak arm and rolls out another of his famous clichés: 'Oh, if Mother could see me now.'

Archon has been designed to excel upwind. Helming her downwind and keeping her hull under the rig in these conditions takes the strength of a weightlifter and the concentration of an archer. I scramble up next to Ron on the helm. His eyes are bloodshot and he is hunched over with exhaustion. In a lull between waves he hands over the helm and I instantly feel the quivering power. *Archon* is alive. Over the last few hours the watch had been taking in sail in response to the building wind; we are now down to our smallest spinnaker and have reduced the mainsail to its second reef.

It takes a good half-hour for the new watch to settle and get over the sensation of being strapped to a runaway freight train. With small movements of the helm I keep *Archon* straight and upright. The sail trimmer, Dean, is as much in control of the boat as I am, and we work together at bleeding the excess power that is driving the boat on.

The wind and seas have now built to the point where we are well overpowered. A larger-than-usual wave rears up astern. *Archon* puts her nose down and takes off. The rig goes slack as tonnes of pressure are released. The wave is now our motive power: we have transitioned from sailing to surfing. The figures on the digital log flick like a pokie machine and rest hard on 25 knots. On each side of us, two walls of green water reach up as the bow wave narrows our focus into a pigeonhole view of the wave ahead. We are in the 'green room', the term used to describe the nirvana of offshore sailors and surfers alike.

Speed is a relative phenomenon. I have been faster on a windsurfer, but that was 100 metres from shore and the comfort of a cold beer and a warm bed. This kind of speed is different. We are on the edge of control, hundreds of miles from help, and the consequences of a wipeout are severe. 'It's no good calling for Mum,' Phil had said as we left the dock in Sydney. His adage aptly summed up the whole caper.

As any surfer will tell you, in the green room time seems to slow down; perhaps it is the focus the pigeonhole view gives you, or perhaps some harking back to the womb. Either way, the on-watch crew are stuck in a trance as we shoot down the wave. The reverie comes to an abrupt halt as we slam into the back of the wave in front and collapse the walls of the green room, which becomes a swoop of white water that rushes over the bow and sweeps Jason off his feet.

Archon charges on helter-skelter, with wave after wave of green-room rides. On the last wave of a big set she takes off with a slight tilt. I have broken the golden rule of keeping the boat under the rig. No amount of strength can stop the inevitable broach, a gentle name for a violent wipeout. This time there is only one wall in the green room. I manage a hoarse, 'Hold on, fellas' as the crew begin scrambling for good holds on a deck that is becoming vertical. We have given up all pretence that we are in control.

Looking along the wave I notice it is beginning to stand up, baring its teeth before it breaks. It is obvious the wave and *Archon* are going to have a dramatic encounter. My brain does a quick, gut-feeling, engineering equation: this looks to be the equivalent of a tiger slapping down a mouse.

Archon meets the towering section of the wave just as it breaks. We hit it at such an angle and with such a speed that the wave flips us upright and slaps the nose of the boat back down the wave. The rig gives an almighty crack as the spinnaker refills. The boat takes off again as if this is just any other wave, shedding green water from her decks like a surfacing U-boat.

There is a prolonged silence as we assume the semblance of control once again. 'Nice whip-bang, skipper,' Jason says, referring to a surfing move fashionable at the time. We quickly reach a unanimous decision to reduce sail and avoid any more whip-bangs.

How we get the spinnaker down without broaching again remains a mystery. Later, the only thing I will remember is the storm jib coming up on deck, ready to replace the spinnaker. It is lashed to the lifelines next to me on the helm. On a small portion of the sail poking out of the bag there is, in Jason's stiff handwriting, 'SHIT! IT'S BLOWING NOW.' Before departure, Jason had been given the job of packing the sails and coding them with a magic marker. It is a bowman's black humour and he is right: we have just gone from racing to survival.

Sometimes, winning means staying in one piece. Slowing down the boat and keeping her balanced to maintain control becomes the aim for the rest of the watch. The seas get bigger by the hour and the wind starts to blow the tops off the waves, leaving a thick salty haze. Occasionally *Archon* surfs down a wave, before decelerating and rolling over the back. During one of these decelerations I look ahead and see a brown hump in the water, just as it passes under our bow. There is an almighty thud as *Archon* stands on her nose, balancing there briefly before rolling on to her port side. We have all been jolted into a pile in the corner of the cockpit. Beside the boat a pilot whale slaps the water with its pectoral fin. The foam around us turns pink with blood. I grab the helm and give it a wiggle to see if the rudder is still there. Below decks the off-watch crew peel up the floorboards to see if the keel bolts are still attached.

'The keel is still on. I can see it,' Jason says, perching over the rail. *Archon* staggers to her feet, picks herself up and sails on as though nothing has happened. Behind us the pilot whale, in its final death throes, quickly disappears between the large waves.

Our watch is done. I pull the hatch shut behind me and kneel, shaking, at the bottom of the companionway steps in a pool of water. Outside, the gale rages on and *Archon* howls in response. In Hobart a tacky trophy with the word *Archon* engraved on it awaits, but for now all that is left is my ragged little soul.

The sail, the play of its
pulse so like our own lives:
so thin and yet so full of
life, so noiseless when it
labours hardest, so noisy
and impatient when least
effective.
HENRY DAVID THOREAU

Solo

AFTER SIX MONTHS of sailing, *Joshua* was close to crossing her outward track around the globe. A rangy Frenchman by the name of Bernard Moitessier was within sight of being the first person to sail solo, non-stop, around the world. Rounding Cape Horn and on his way north up the Atlantic, he fired a message by slingshot on to the deck of a passing tanker. It read: 'I am continuing non-stop because I am happy at sea and perhaps because I want to save my soul.' He changed course to the east and sailed into obscurity.

A few months later an Englishman by the name of Knox-Johnston and his tubby 32-foot ketch *Suhaili* took the prize, while another English solo sailor stepped off his boat deep in the North Atlantic and disappeared.

Sailing solo over long distances is a strange game. It requires a curious mix: the practical seaman and the starry-eyed dreamer. In today's world the starry-eyed element has been eclipsed by the glory of competition. Yet, underneath the sponsorship endorsements and live internet tracking, the dreamer still survives in a forgotten corner of sailing's soul.

New Zealand has never made much of our solo sailors, confining them to the fringes with the artists, the poets and the birders. Perhaps it's the result of the antipodean penchant for team sports, or a suspicion that anyone who wants to spend time alone on the ocean is queer in the head. In France it's different: being outrageously queer in the head is something to celebrate. Solo sailing is the pinnacle of the French yachting world and the sailors are lauded as rock stars. To sail alone is very much part of the French's perception of who they are.

The father of French solo sailing was Alain Gerbault. He was a dreamer of the first order, and like painter Paul Gauguin before him he was obsessed with escaping the ills of the modern world. He had much to escape from as he was a decorated war hero and French tennis champion. He attracted publicity at every turn and was constantly lauded by high society everywhere he went in Europe. This made him sick to his stomach, so much so that his leaky old cutter *Firecrest* and the lagoons of far-flung islands of the South Pacific seemed preferable to life ashore.

Most sailing narratives of the era were boringly descriptive and practical. Gerbault's book *In Quest of the Sun* stood out for its boldly articulated dreams, and its hint that sailing solo might be good for the spirit. The book became an instant best-seller, and to Gerbault's displeasure made him more famous than ever.

In Quest of the Sun became the favourite reading of Bernard Moitessier when he was growing up in a region of the obscure colony of French Indochina now known as Vietnam. His upbringing was a classic slice of 1940s French colonial life: pleasant, narrow and conservative. Despite this, Moitessier showed a passion for the sea, the jungle and the Asian art of simple living. By the age of 26 he had had enough of his restrictive world. He dropped out and headed off to sea well before either of those ideas became fashionable.

Through his youth he had sampled a taste of the spiritual side of seafaring. He had spent his summers tagging along with the fishermen of the Gulf of Siam and begun to pick up on their ideas of the sea. To the Vietnamese fishermen of the time the sea was a place of magic and their boats were as sacred as temples. Something of this spirit entered Moitessier and never left him.

His early boats were junks and badly built timber yachts. Funds were perpetually short and he learnt through necessity such desperate measures as recaulking a leaky carvel boat with a bucket of sawdust released under water.

Over 15 years of frugal adventures, Moitessier walked away from two shipwrecks and a rotten hulk with nothing but his clothes. After each disaster he built another boat and slowly began to shape his vision of the perfect offshore yacht.

In 1958, after the wreck of his third boat, *Marie-Thérèse II*, in the Caribbean, Moitessier managed to find his way back to France, where he came dangerously close to settling for a normal life as a pharmaceutical salesman. What saved him was the publication of his first book, *Sailing to the Reefs*. Like *In Quest of the Sun*, this book touched a nerve in a whole new audience of would-be blue-water sailors who were thirsty for the spirit of the sea.

It also got him noticed by a prominent French naval architect called Jean Knocker. Out of the ruins of his previous boats, Moitessier and Knocker designed *Joshua*, a 39-foot steel, double-ended ketch. *Joshua* and Moitessier were destined to become one of the sailing world's great duos.

Moitessier's sailing of *Joshua* non-stop, two-handed, 14,216 nautical miles from Tahiti to Alicante, France, via Cape Horn was perhaps the first time the world took note of the bold Frenchman and his red yacht. The journey set Moitessier up as a pre-eminent offshore sailor and proved *Joshua* as a fast and strong vessel, superbly suited to the testing conditions of the Southern Ocean. While Moitessier was out testing his limits, the rest of the sailing world sat around sipping gin and talking about it.

In 1967, as a result of the interest stirred by Francis Chichester's two-part solo circumnavigation, the Sunday Times Golden Globe Race was conceived. A prize of a Golden Globe and £5,000 were offered to the first non-stop solo circumnavigation and the fastest time respectively. This stirred the imagination of a number of sailors but all eyes were on Moitessier.

When Moitessier chose to compete in the race, the dreamer and the pragmatic sailor within him were forced to confront each other. The dreamer despised the idea of competing, while the pragmatist knew he could do it successfully. Moitessier stood head and shoulders above the other competitors, who had neither the experience nor the boat for the job. He took the challenge reluctantly but his voyage was destined to become an epic of seamanship.

When he fired his message by slingshot on to the deck of a passing freighter, the Frenchman shocked the sailing world. What awaited him, had he continued northward up the Atlantic, was a heady mixture of money and fame. Moitessier wanted none of it. He had achieved a Zen-like state that would take him one and a half times around the world and into anonymity.

On the surface his actions may have looked like those of a madman. However, Moitessier was far from mad. He had reached that state of wanting to sail forever that is not uncommon in offshore sailors. The only difference was that he acted on the sensation, and was smart enough to know that the fame and fortune that awaited him, had he completed the race, would have destroyed his life.

Most of the other competitors in the Golden Globe race were ill-prepared Englishmen. Perhaps the most astonishing of these was Donald Crowhurst. Crowhurst's preparation, in stark contrast to Moitessier's, was a shambles. The perfect combination of lack of experience, an unsuitable boat and crushing financial woes meant Crowhurst's attempt at the race was destined to be a stunning failure.

Nicholas Tomalin and Ron Hall's book *The Strange Last Voyage of Donald Crowhurst* chronicles the crumbling of a mind under immense pressure. Not long into the race Crowhurst realised that his chances of winning or even finishing were slim. Unfortunately he needed to win as he faced certain bankruptcy on his return. He devised an ingenious scam whereby he would sail around the Atlantic in *Teignmouth Electron* while putting out false position statements that had him circling the world. As the false positions caught up with the real positions in the Atlantic he would rejoin the race for real and claim the prize.

He developed a two-book system of keeping his log, one book for the imaginary voyage and the other for the real. While the imaginary one was boring as hell, the real one was a fascinating record of the disintegration of his mind.

Somewhere in the North Atlantic, Crowhurst realised there was no way out of his scam. Obsessed with time and God, he became, according to his log, a cosmic being. In the great English tradition of glorious failure, he stepped off his boat at exactly 11.20 Greenwich Mean Time with a chronometer in his hand and an appointment with God. The last lines he scrawled in his real log were 'it is finished, it is finished. IT IS THE MERCY'.

As *Teignmouth Electron* sailed on under mizzen without Crowhurst, Moitessier was nearing Tahiti after ten months at sea and 35,000 nautical miles under the keel. By doing the incomprehensible and opting out while in the lead, Moitessier was labelled a dreamer and consigned to the scrapheap by the sailing world. For his remaining years he lived a vagabond existence based on 'Ahe, an atoll in the Tuamotus, an archipelago in French Polynesia. He tried normal things such as having a family, but would obsessively up sticks and head to sea for indeterminate periods of time, as if trying to recapture his communion with the ocean.

It all ended as it had begun. In 1985 *Joshua* was caught in a freak storm and wrecked on the beach of Cabo San Lucas in Mexico. Moitessier's heart was broken and he gave his beloved boat to a couple of young Californians, who restored her and eventually sold her to La Rochelle's Maritime Museum in the south of France. Moitessier built another boat and wrote prolifically but it seemed the magic was gone. In 1994 he quietly died of cancer.

Late one French summer I came across *Joshua* at the La Rochelle Boat Show. She lay in an obscure corner of the marina among the schlocky fibreglass and stainless steel. Moitessier would have been disgusted by the opulence and waste around *Joshua*, with boats designed like caravans and not with the sea in mind at all. Her bright red dented hull was at odds with all that, yet there was a long queue snaking down the walkway. I waited my turn and slipped aboard.

Everything about *Joshua* had Moitessier's hand of simplicity, from the telegraph pole masts to the faithful block and tackle he used before he could afford winches. I visited her many more times during the boat show and each time I sat on her deck I could see the reverence with which the French regarded her.

Moitessier's books have been reprinted many times and today they are read more than ever. Some of the crowd on the dock clutched copies while waiting patiently with lowered voices and peaceful stares: *Joshua* and her erstwhile owner seemed to demand the kind of respect usually reserved for victors. In the years following his decision to opt out, Moitessier had quietly become a hero and *Joshua* the shrine for a nation that loves its sailors and dreamers.

There is but a plank
between a sailor
and eternity.
THOMAS GIBBONS

Deep six

EVERY SAILOR HAS an inventory of things lost overboard. These lists are occasionally compared as a sort of scorecard in a game the sea always wins. Over my time at sea I have involuntarily deposited four hats, two winch handles and a watch. While this may be a trivial list, it is a good reminder that the sea is in charge of the game. Only on rare occasions are these small trifles ever given back, and if they are they are salt-worn and immediately cast aside, as if the sea has removed some vital spark.

Throwing stuff over the side of boats has been around since day one. At their heart, sailors are minimalists, or perhaps it is the sea that demands everything superfluous must be sacrificed. A yacht is the one place where you can be free from the clutter that swamps a life on land.

To jettison anything from a boat is often referred to as to 'deep-six' it. The expression has something to do with six feet to the fathom and watching the object sink from the light into that dark space between the boat and the underworld below. While the expression is more metaphorical than actual in these days of environmental consciousness, it still maintains its currency with sailors.

While most things on a boat can be deep-sixed, this never applies to the crew. There are those who, like Donald Crowhurst, want to jump off a boat, but they are thankfully an insane minority. For the rest of us, falling off a boat is a cardinal sin that can be likened to a climber letting go of a mountain.

Like every cardinal rule there are fables to back it up. In the days of the clipper ships rounding Cape Horn, on their way back to Europe from the Pacific, to fall overboard was considered terminal. In the gales that lashed the high latitudes the captain of a fully rigged clipper could barely contemplate turning around and bashing back upwind to save some poor wretch – so much so that it was a standing order on some ships to sail on.

To lose your grip in the rigging was to lose your grip on life itself. It is said that in one such instance a ship's boy who fell from a clipper running hard downwind in the Southern Ocean was miraculously spotted and picked up by another that was close behind it. The sailors on the rescuing clipper, *Sobraon*, listened with superstition to the boy's incredible story. They let him finish and then promptly hanged him from the rigging, suspecting he was a ghost.

To fall into the heart of the sea and return is a rare thing. There is a belief, clearly espoused by the crew of the *Sobraon*, that whoever returns is not the same person: although they swan around with the living they have been privy to the thoughts of the dead.

Tony Lister is the only sailor I have known to do this thing. For years he has voyaged from my home port in his baby-blue Piver trimaran *Corsair*. To sail with Tony is to experience sailing as ritual. His boat handling is impeccable and his knowledge of a certain patch of water impressive. On board he has only one cassette tape, *Neil Diamond's Greatest Hits*, which he plays while underway. If you are going to have only one album, I guess Neil's is as good as any.

Tony's ritual is to sail *Corsair* up the coast and offshore against a building sea breeze. By three o'clock the breeze is at its peak, and like clockwork *Corsair* is tacked around, the spinnaker set, and a roller-coaster ride home ensues. More often than not Tony is sailing by himself with only Hector's dolphins and Neil Diamond for company.

Every summer weekend for 30 years Tony has enjoyed this ritual, but as is the nature of the sea it is always different. One late summer's afternoon around three o'clock Tony tacked *Corsair*, put on the auto helm, and went forward to set up the spinnaker for hoisting. He had done this thousands of times before but on this occasion a wave knocked him off his feet and into the water. He surfaced in time to see *Corsair* sail off by herself.

Just then Tony had three things going for him: he was conscious, he was wearing a life vest, and people knew his ritual.

Tony's wife Erica kept in regular radio contact with him when he sailed, so when he missed his call and would not answer his cell phone the search began. For five hours Tony floated in the sea, inching his way to the beach through the heavy folds of a big south swell. An armada of boats and aircraft eventually tracked him down before sundown. The pilot boat that Tony worked on during the week picked him up in an advanced state of hypothermia.

To meet Tony today you would not suspect this cheerful man has peeked into the gates of hell. When I met him a while after his ordeal I wanted to say welcome back, but could not find the words. Like the other sailors who knew him, I could not help thinking it could have been me.

My mind hovers briefly on Tony and his ordeal as I lean on *Siward*'s chart table, filling in the logbook before heading ashore for the night. The month of May has an edge to it in the south, doing an impersonation of winter that is very convincing. In the cabin the warm timber lit by kerosene lamp is taking the edge off the cold.

As always, I feel reluctant to leave *Siward*, to travel back to the world of work and bills to pay. Her mooring is only a few hundred metres from the shore yet it is enough distance to keep that world at bay. My mind flits over Tony and then moves on to other topics of procrastination, as it is prone to do when faced with going back ashore.

It is getting on to nightfall as I slope my way through the routine of leaving, starting at the bow and working my way to the stern, switching off sea cocks and batteries, and double-lashing halyards so they do not bang on the mast. Better this than waking in the night realising you have left a porthole open or a battery on, the thought gnawing a hole in your sleep until you eventually row out and fix the problem.

My ritual ends at the stern as this is the easiest stepping-off point. It also means I can spin around and do a quick mental check to see if I have missed anything.

In the dim light astern waits *Siward*'s tender, a skittish white rowing dinghy I picked up for a song. Stepping off *Siward* into the dinghy entails another ritual, which, like the others, is automatic. This one is simple but requires dexterity: I need to hook the painter with my foot, spin the dinghy around, and step in on the centre line. Perhaps my thoughts have drifted to the responsibilities of the land as I hook the painter with my foot, spin the dinghy around and step into the dingy just off-centre. The dinghy skids away and I am in the sea.

The cold makes me gasp. It hurts. My gasping sucks in water and I begin to splutter. I reach out for something to hold me up but *Siward*'s smooth hull may as well be an iceberg. Her beautiful curves offer no handholds. My down-filled jacket quickly becomes leaden and amplifies the crushing feeling of lack of breath. As it begins to suck me down I unzip it and do something like a forward roll under the water to slide out of its embrace.

Surfacing next to *Siward* I realise I have done it now. The shore is well out of my range and the other boats around also offer only smooth-sided hulls. The dinghy lies astern, upside down and a foot or so under water. I spend the next twenty minutes attempting ever more desperate ways to clamber back aboard *Siward*. A rising surge of anger begins boiling up in me: this is how I will go and it is so senseless. There is going to be no peaceful walk into the light.

As the bitter cold takes grip I feel my body slowly shutting up shop. My arms and legs begin to feel wooden as the blood surges inward to protect my vital organs. My mind slowly drifts into a wet fogginess, giving me the sensation of being a spectator.

Through this haze I have noticed that *Siward* is lying side on to the short chop that is curving into the bay. This makes her dip her rail occasionally, as if curtsying to the sea. At the lowest point of her sheer-line on the leeward side, I position myself ready for the next dip. I have a keen sense that, given my dwindling reserves of strength, this is my last chance. To hold your life in your own cold hands, even for a minute, is an immense thing. Time insists you rapidly snatch it back or let it go.

Anger propels me out of the water and I hook my fingers over *Siward*'s rail. Once there, I use my body weight to gently rock the boat in time with the chop, waiting for an extra-long roll. *Siward* dips her rail towards me and hesitates for a second. With one almighty heave I manage to get the crook of my arm around a stanchion and my knee locked over the gunwale. With each successive back roll I use the momentum to inch my way further aboard. A calf, a rib, an elbow: I ratchet my way up the side until I can roll under the lifelines and on to the deck.

My body does not feel like mine. I am beyond walking and can only slither my way back to the cabin, down the companionway and on to the chart table. My hands have long since sacrificed their blood to my body's core. I knock the radio microphone off its hook and jam the transmit button by sliding it with my stiff arms into the edge of the chart table.

Someone must have heard my garbled message for not long afterwards, weak as a kitten, I am picked up by a fellow sailor. He lowers me into his inflatable dinghy and takes me to the cruising club. Among the sailors enjoying an after-race drink is an intensive care nurse, who gently brings me back to life with draughts of warm water. Heat gradually spreads back to my periphery, allowing me to feel and think and re-enter the land of the living. Slowly the warmth pulls a veil over what I have seen between the living and the dead.

I tell only close friends of my experience, using expressions such as 'a bit of a swim'. They take it in good humour and ask me if it is time to quit the sea. 'Not in a million years,' I say.

I do a great job of pretending I am the same person. On the outside the only noticeable changes are my religious use of a life vest on the water and a new dinghy for *Siward*. I sell the skittish one for a song and replace it with a sturdier, more stable model.

One sharp-witted friend says, 'You deep-sixed yourself.' He is right. I added my life to my small inventory of jettisoned possessions and was lucky enough to get it back, cold and salt-worn from the sea.

*Indeed the cruising of a
boat here and there is very
much what happens to the
soul of man in a larger way.
We set out for places we do
not reach, or reach too late;
and on the way, there befall
us all manner of things
which we could never have
awaited.*

HILAIRE BELLOC

Six green men, and other guests

I WAS NEARING THE END of myself. It was my fourth day without sleep as we raced *Archon* across the Tasman Sea in a gale. There had been never-ending sail changes and a violent motion that meant sleep had been impossible. For the last day now, each time I closed my eyes a dream rolled, as if the projectionist in my head had been waiting for his cue. As I opened my eyes the dream would abruptly stop and the ferocity of the gale would rush back in to fill the void.

It is said that you can go without sleep for some time. However, you cannot go without dreaming. It's as if the mind demands time to sort itself out and digest the meaning of the day. I was at the point where my mind was demanding to dream and to hell with the day. The fact I needed a good chunk of my wits to keep *Archon* straight before the seas seemed the least pressing of the demands placed upon me.

We were near the end of the gale, and as there were no sail changes required only Dean and I were on deck. I helmed and Dean trimmed the sails in an unspoken stupor. We were in the dark hours before dawn, and a glorious display of phosphorescence was turning our wake and every breaking wave into a glowing beard of light.

The dreams that had waited patiently for me to close my eyes now surged over the wall that normally prevented them swamping my waking mind. A bigger wave than usual crashed across the deck, lighting up *Archon* in a phosphorescent blaze. I closed my eyes to avoid the familiar sting of salt water and opened them to see six human-like figures made of luminous green phosphorescence scrambling back down the deck. All glowing form and no features, they hunkered down in the cockpit, being sure to fit around the winches, ropes and Dean, who was busy trimming the mainsail. They had the cordiality of a familiar crew, chatting and joking among themselves, and I felt I knew them well.

I knew I was not going mad, that this was merely an illusion conjured up by severe sleep deprivation. If anything, it was a great comfort to have these visions aboard.

The gale raged on despite them, as did the workings of *Archon*. We chatted with a warm familiarity, and even paused as we took off on tricky waves that required my total concentration on the helm. The details of the conversation are lost to me now. However, I remember a welcome sense of reassurance that I was going to be okay and that they were proud of me, not just out there in the Tasman Sea but in my life as a whole.

We spoke for some time in low whispers before the cheery group bade me farewell, clambering out of the cockpit and up to the bow. Another large wave crashed on deck and they were gone.

With just the whisker of a suspicion it might all have been real, I yelled over the wind to Dean, 'Did you see that?' 'See what?' he replied.

At the end of our watch, despite the still violent motion I collapsed into my bunk and slept like the dead for the first time in four days. When I awoke the gale had abated and I felt an overwhelming sense of lightness.

Later, as we neared Sydney Heads, I told Dean of my waking dream. He grinned, took a long drag on his cigarette and said, 'The least the buggers could have done is changed up to the number three headsail before they left.'

Having folk, phosphorescent or otherwise, aboard for a sail is one of the great pleasures of owning a boat. Entertaining guests creates a Noah's Ark of good humour and easy company, and is an excellent way to share your kingdom with people you like. It is one of the few instances where you can select good people over all the other types who have to be tolerated in your life on land.

On *Siward* the event begins with a simple statement: 'Come for a sail with us.' This is more than a mere invitation: it is a ticket to a kingdom. Like all good invitations it is not issued out of desperation: *Siward* is a good cruising boat and can easily be handled alone. It is offered in recognition of the quality of the company.

More often than not, my guests are landlubbers curious about the sea. Once aboard they will exude the faintest hint of terror. They will nervously spin the winches, poke their nose briefly down the main hatchway, and then take up position in the cockpit, where they will remain for the rest of the day. After a time they will begin to relax and take the helm. At some stage in the late afternoon I will hint that we must run for home. At this suggestion they will suddenly develop the demeanour of reluctant children.

Some who come aboard become regulars. They assume their favourite position, either in the galley with a tea towel over their shoulder, producing endless streams of nice food, or hogging the helm. They are comfortable with the ritual of sailing and nearly as addicted to it as the owner. Some of this mob get to experience overnight trips to favourite bays, where there are conversations deep into the night by the glow of a kerosene lamp.

On land they are electricians, landscape architects and psychiatrists, yet none of that seems to matter when they step aboard. They shed a skin or two and immerse themselves in the nation of the boat. We become a small community with simple rules to live by.

Observing the reactions of first-time sailors aboard *Siward* is a delight. I have witnessed responses to the first puff of wind and surge of the helm that range from complete euphoria to virtual collapse. All of these reactions are honest, and all allow a brief peek at the person beneath the skin.

Each guest will, without asking, bring something for the boat. Mainly it is food and drink. Anything not consumed by the crew will go into the kitty, like an offering left at a shrine. Most will be subsequently consumed by other guests, the exception being a bottle of rough brandy that seemed to last forever until it was found that mixing it into a hot Milo on a cold day made it just drinkable.

There is coffee in a tube, which says more about the ability of condensed milk to make anything taste good than about the coffee. There is also a beautiful smell of oiled timber wafting around the cabin, and if you spend long enough on board this aroma will get into your clothes and hair so that after a time you will smell like the boat.

Perhaps the most confusing aspect of the statement 'Come for a sail with us' is the 'us'. Referring to my sailing self in the plural is an odd habit I have picked up, as more often than not I sail *Siward* alone. On occasion the plurality causes great confusion to my guests. When they come aboard, their eyes dart around the boat looking for my imaginary friends.

On one memorable occasion the confusion produced an unusual result. Nancy, a friend of a friend from Canada who had answered the invitation to come for a sail with us, had assumed 'us' meant my wife and family and had brought enough food for six. I had assumed that, like most of my friends, Nancy would come as a pair.

When Nancy came aboard there was a brief awkward moment as she and I looked for wives, husbands and children. I sheepishly explained the 'us' thing, expecting she would leap back on to the wharf. Instead she burst out laughing and her blues eyes sparkled. Up until then I had viewed dates as only slightly less scary than a full-blown storm at sea and had done my best to avoid both. With Nancy's warm laugh, however, it seemed we were on an accidental date, the absurdity of which meant any chance of shyness or fear evaporated.

We had a delightful north-east sea breeze and all day to explore the harbour. I gave Nancy the helm and busied myself making cups of tea and trimming the sails. I could see delight spreading across her face as the first gentle puffs of wind heeled *Siward* and sent a soft hiss out in the wake behind. In between tacks we talked of our families, of Canada and its similarities to New Zealand, of sailing, of *Siward*, and of our mutual friends. We snacked on enough good food for six, using mismatched plastic plates and cutlery that may have been used to mix up epoxy resin at some stage. At some point we rowed ashore and climbed a hill and kept talking.

It was twilight before we were back on the mooring. Nancy was as reluctant as I was to leave the boat and go back on shore. I had my head down in the cockpit clearing up the tangle of ropes that had accumulated while we sailed, when I chanced to look up. She was gazing back at me from up by the mast. Her eyes were the blue that a tropical ocean of a certain depth goes in bright sunlight, the kind of blue that makes you want to dive in. On the edge of the blue there was a faint hint of phosphorescence.

*For all your constantly
making for it, the horizon
stays at the same distance,
right at hand and out
of reach. Yet deep down
you know that the way
covered is all that counts.*
BERNARD MOITESSIER

The same
ocean twice

I T HAD BEEN a different ocean and I
had been a different man the last time
I sailed there. I had memories of the
voyage to Tonga in *Manaroa III* but
only fragments remained, such as the soft warm trade
winds and the galaxy of phosphorescence spreading out
in our wake at night.

Of all the parties to celebrate our arrival it's the one at
Aisea's Beach I remember most vividly. It involved a dis-
orderly collection of yachts rafted up together. The crew
moved from boat to boat, following the shade and the
food. The talk revolved around gales, reefs, and scoun-
drels we all knew. It was soaked in a slow trickle of rum.

I was too young and fit for endurance drinking to be my strong point. During the day I would escape the party, swim ashore, and spend my time chatting to an old hermit in a copra hut on the beach, or hiding from the afternoon sun on the porch of a church, listening to the waft of the congregation at full volume. The Tongans I met on my wanderings would inevitably ask their standard question: 'Where's your family?' My standard reply would be to smile and point south to New Zealand, and pretend not to notice their looks of concern.

After three days at Aisea's Beach we ran out of booze. The party dried up and the yachts departed, with promises to keep in touch shouted across the water. The promises dissolved as our land lives took over once more, and we returned to being farmers and students and second-hand car salesmen.

I did a lot of reading on that voyage, from an impressive collection of dangerous books, mostly by sailors such as Johnny Wray, Bernard Moitessier and Alain Gerbault. On my off watch I would lose myself in their chapters, which filled the vast swathe of the Pacific Ocean that surrounded us. Occasionally I would rest, place the book on my chest, watch the moonlight sweep across the cabin of *Manaroa III* with every roll, and marvel at my own adventure.

The stories of these sailors became like crosses on my chart of the ocean, each adding to a growing reservoir of memories. I remember also chewing through *An*

Introduction to Early Greek Philosophy: it was here I came across Heraclitus, the weeping philosopher. Many of his great thoughts have been lost but one of the fragments that remains is: 'You cannot step in the same river twice.' He qualifies this by adding: 'It is not the same river, nor is it the same man.'

If Heraclitus had been a sailor he would have included oceans in the proverb. Sixteen years later, and despite his sage advice, I attempted to cross the same ocean twice. Night was falling and from the anchorage at Aisea's Beach it did not look as though much had changed. A mix of distance and low light was obscuring the details, but the quiet presence of the place was still there. I put off going ashore until the morning, content to be with Nancy and my dreams of the past, and fearing a closer inspection would reveal unwelcome changes.

As the years had rolled on I had continued to be unzipped by the sea. I had examined my stuffing, discarding the fluff and keeping the true bits that only the sea and I might know. I had raced for tacky trophies and cruised until the rat effect set in. I had fallen in love with a boat of my own and fallen off her. She had become part of my name in the bay, and I had learned how to care for her and her occasional crew. I had conjured up land from the sea ahead. I had taught others the joy of sailing and had had many guests aboard. I had sought reassurance in a waking dream of phosphorescent friends and, more frighteningly, found the real thing in a guest with swimming-pool eyes. I had married her and we had visited our favourite places together. I had told her of Tonga and the voyage in *Manaroa III*. She had smiled and said, 'We should go there.'

As Heraclitus had predicted, things had changed — with the ocean and the sailor. Gone were the dense bush and the copra hut with its lone occupant. Instead there was a derelict pearl farm and a rough concrete wharf, abandoned except for a couple of kids swimming off a rusty ladder.

There were changes onboard as well. Nancy was pregnant with our first child. Time was precious. Instead of sailing from New Zealand we had flown to Tonga, avoiding gales and reefs, and trading the intensity of an offshore passage for the convenience of a chartered yacht.

From the deck of the yacht I could see that the beach was deserted: there were no three-day parties. Nancy's swimming-pool eyes were closed in a deep sleep. I quietly rowed ashore in the morning calm, curious to see what remained of my memories. I slid to within metres of the beach, stopped and leaned on my oars. Above me, the kids peered down from the dilapidated wharf, their dark eyes wide with questions. They stared without pause, as small children do. We hovered, gazing at each other, while the sea gurgled around the pilings of the wharf.

'Where's your family?' chirped the smallest. I pointed to the yacht. Heraclitus was right: some things had changed. I smiled. I wept.

Dangerous books

Where possible, the most recent paperback edition of each book is given.

The £200 Millionaire, Weston Martyr: Rupert Hart-Davies, 1961

Adlard Coles' Heavy Weather Sailing, Peter Bruce: Adlard Coles Nautical, 2008

Blake's Odyssey: The Round the World Race with Ceramco New Zealand, Peter Blake and Alan Sefton: Hodder & Stoughton, 1982

Bluewater Vagabond: Six Years' Adventure at Sea, Dennis Puleston: Rupert Hart-Davis, 1955

The Boy Who Sailed Around the World Alone, Robin Lee Graham: Golden Press, 1974

The Capable Cruiser, Lin Pardey and Larry Pardey: Pardey Books, 2010

The Cruise of the Dream Ship, Ralph Stock: W. Heinemann, 1950

The Cruise of the Teddy, Erling Tambs: Grafton Books, 1989

Cruising Under Sail, Eric Hiscock: Adlard Coles Nautical, 1991

Desperate Voyage, John Caldwell: Sheridan House, 1991

Ice Bird: The Classic Story of the First Single-handed Voyage to Antarctica, David Lewis: Adlard Coles Nautical, 2002

In Quest of the Sun, Alain Gerbault: Hodder & Stoughton, 1937

The Long Way, Bernard Moitessier: Sheridan House, 1995

'Mischief in Patagonia' in *The Eight Sailing/Mountain-Exploration Books*, H.W. Tilman: Hodder & Stoughton, 1989

North to the Night: A Spiritual Odyssey in the Arctic, Alvah Simon: Broadway Books, 1999

Once is Enough, Miles Sweeton: Grafton Books, 1984

Painted Ocean, Neil Arrow: Caxton Press, 1961

Sailing Alone Around the World, Captain Joshua Slocum: CreateSpace Independent Publishing Platform, 2011

Sailing to the Reefs, Bernard Moitessier: Sheridan House, 2001

The Sailor's World, Arthur Beiser: Ridge Press, 1978

'The Sea and the Wind that Blows' in *Essays of E.B. White*, E.B. White: Harper Perennial Modern Classics, 2006

Selected Novels and Stories: Joseph Conrad: Hamlyn, 1986

Sheila in the Wind, Adrian Hayter: Lodestar Books, 2013

Shrimpy: A Record Round-the-world Voyage in an 18-Foot Yacht, Shane Acton: Patrick Stephens, 1993

South Sea Vagabonds, Johnny Wray: Grafton Books, 1988

The Strange Last Voyage of Donald Crowhurst, Nicholas Tomalin and Ron Hall: McGraw Hill, 2003

Swallows and Amazons, Arthur Ransome: Vintage Children's Classics, 2012

Swirly World: The Solo Voyages, Andrew Fagan: Harper Collins, 2001

There Be No Dragons: How to Cross a Big Ocean in a Small Sailboat, Reese Palley: Sheridan House, 2004

Towards Banks Peninsula, Denis Glover: Pegasus Press, 1979

Trekka Round the World, John Guzzwell: Fine Edge, 1999

The Venturesome Voyages of Captain Voss, J.C. Voss: Benediction Classics, 2011

A Voyage for Madmen, Peter Nichols: Profile Books, 2011

Voyaging on a Small Income, Annie Hill: Thomas Reed Publications, 2001

Voyaging the Pacific: In Search of the South, Miles Hordern: John Murray, 2003

We, the Navigators: The Ancient Art of Landfinding in the Pacific, David Lewis: University of Hawai'i Press, 1994

The Wind is Free, Frank Wrightman: Panther Books, 1956

A World of My Own: The First Ever Non-stop Solo Round the World Voyage, Robin Knox-Johnston: Adlard Coles Nautical, 2004

Glossary

aft   Towards the stern (or back section) of a vessel.

alongside   By the side of a wharf or boat.

backstay   Long wires, reaching from the stern of the vessel to the masthead, used to support the mast.

barometer   Instrument for measuring barometric pressure.

boom   Spar that supports the lowest horizontal section of a sail.

bow   Front of a boat.

broach   When a sailing vessel loses control of its motion and is forced into a sudden sharp turn, often heeling heavily and, in smaller vessels, sometimes leading to a capsize.

capsize   When a boat leans too far and rolls over, exposing the keel or centreboard.

catamaran Boat made up of two hulls.

centreline Imaginary line down the centre of a vessel lengthwise.

centreboard Small retractable keel, usually without ballast.

cruising Art of sailing for relaxation.

cutter Single-masted boat, with two or more headsails.

double ender Boat that has a stern shaped like a bow.

dragging Action of dragging the anchor across the bottom, causing the boat to drift.

ebb Outward phase of the tide.

gaff-rigged Boat rigged with a four-sided sail with its upper edge supported by a spar, or gaff, that extends aft from the mast.

galley Kitchen of a ship.

green flash Last flash of sunlight as the sun drops below the horizon at sea.

gybe Change from one tack to the other away from the wind, with the stern of the vessel turning through the wind.

jib Triangular sail at the front of a yacht.

keel Central structural basis of a hull, shaped as a foil to aid windward travel.

ketch Two-masted yacht with the smaller a shorter aft mast (mizzen) stepped in front of the rudder.

knot Unit of speed: 1 nautical mile (1.8520 kilometres; 1.1508 miles) per hour.

landlubber Person unfamiliar with being on the sea.

lee-oh Command given to tack through the wind.

life vest Flotation device that allows freedom of movement for the wearer. Not to be confused with life jacket.

lines Ropes for mooring. Also, the shape of a yacht's hull.

luff Forward edge of a sail.

mainsail Larger sail aft of the mast on a yacht.

mainsheet Rope and blocks that connect to the boom, which allow trimming of the mainsail.

marina Docking facility for yachts and launches.

moor Attach a boat to a mooring buoy or post.

nautical mile Unit of length corresponding approximately to one minute of latitude; by international agreement it is exactly 1,852 metres.

phosphorescence Heatless light generated chemically by marine plants and animals stimulated in the surface layers of the sea.

pitch Vessel's motion that causes the fore and aft ends to rise and fall repetitively.

pitchpole Capsize a boat stern over bow, rather than by rolling over.

planing When a fast-moving vessel skims over the water instead of pushing through it.

plumb bow Bow that drops straight to the water without curve or rake.

port Left-hand side of a vessel when the vessel is facing forward.

reaching Sailing at 90° to the wind.

reefing Temporarily reducing the area of a sail exposed to the wind, usually to guard against adverse effects of strong wind or to slow the vessel.

seacock Valve in the hull of a boat.

sheer Upward curve of a vessel's longitudinal lines as viewed from the side.

sloop Yacht with one mast bearing a mainsail and a headsail/jib.

spinnaker Large sail flown in front of the vessel while heading downwind.

starboard Right-hand side of a vessel when the vessel is facing forward.

stern Back of a boat.

tack Change direction by steering the bow of the boat through the wind.

tiller Steering arm of a yacht, connected to the rudder.

trimaran Vessel with three hulls.

trimming Adjusting the angle of the sails to the wind.

wake Turbulence behind a vessel.

whip bang Surfing move that involves hitting the breaking section of a wave to redirect the board back down the wave.

yawl Yacht with two masts, main and mizzen, the mizzen being stepped behind the rudderpost.

ACKNOWLEDGEMENTS

For kicking open the front door for me I would like to thank Rebecca Priestley. For letting me in the door I thank Mary Varnham and the staff of Awa Press. For literary encouragement I would like to thank Steve Braunias, Owen Marshall and Alice Miller. Thanks, too, to my excellent readers Jenny Agnew, Nancy Vance, Murray Vance and Doreen Vance; to my family for their unconditional support; to the sailors I have met and learned much from, including the crews of *Chance*, *Spodian*, *Whispering Hope*, *Gambero*, *Corsair*, *Sheena*, *Archon*, *Big Don't Argue*, *Smokey*, *Manaroa III*, *The Shag*, *Crystal Voyage*, *Safari*, *Corylus*, *Smuggler*, *Siward*, *Party Time*, *Huia*, *Carly*, *Siren*, *Backlash*, *Temptation* and *Windflower*; to the authors of the dangerous books, and to all those who have shared with me their passion for the sea.

If you enjoyed this book, you may also like these from the award-winning series.

How to Watch a Game of Rugby
Spiro Zavos

978-0-9582509-3-1

> 'One for all rugby lovers ...
> Spiro Zavos's best book yet'
> **Bryce Courtenay**

Celebrated rugby writer Spiro Zavos shares his passion for the perfect game, and tackles some of the great mysteries: Did the Greeks invent rugby? Should players have pre-match sex? Which US president played fullback at Yale? An eye-opener for both rugby fans and those who don't know a ruck from a maul – yet.

How to Gaze at the Southern Stars
Richard Hall

978-0-9582509-9-3

> 'Will beguile experienced star-spotters and
> absolute beginners alike'
> *New Scientist*

Come on a tour of the heavens with astronomer extraordinaire Richard Hall. In this popular book, the founder of the acclaimed science centre Stonehenge Aotearoa weaves state-of-the-art science with the stories and myths of peoples across the globe and through the centuries. The night sky will never look the same again.

THE GINGER SERIES

Captivating Reads for Curious People

How to Drink a Glass of Wine
John Saker

978-0-9582538-2-6

'If you're going to read only one book about wine,
make it this one' *Cuisine*

A glass of wine is the simplest of pleasures – elixir of love, soothing balm and forger of friendships. Yet wine is also the product of good fruit gone bad, a mosaic of smells, tastes and textures, and a highly competitive international industry. In this book you will learn about wine's strange aromas, the odd history of many vines, peculiar practices in wineries, who decides if a wine is a winner, how the shape of a glass can change the taste, and many more secrets of the trade.

How to Look at a Painting
Justin Paton

978-1-877551-29-1

Winner
Montana Book Award for Contemporary Culture
Best Art Book of the Year
Listener, The Press, The Dominion Post
Major 12-part television series

In this brilliant book, acclaimed art writer Justin Paton takes us on a journey of exploration through the centuries and across the painted world – from the luscious fruit of Italy's Caravaggio to the lonely landscapes of New Zealand's Rita Angus, the dazzling panoramas of America's Lari Pittman and the mysterious 'tombstones' of Japan's On Kawara.

Available from all good bookstores and online at
www.awapress.com

How to Watch a Bird
Steve Braunias

978-0-9582629-6-5

> 'A small and perfectly formed jewel'
> *The Sunday Star-Times*

As prize-winning journalist Steve Braunias stands on an apartment balcony on a sultry summer evening a black-backed gull flies so close he is instantaneously bowled over with happiness. 'I thought: Birds, everywhere. I wanted to know more about them.' This book is the result – a moving personal journey into an amazing world.

How to Play a Video Game
Pippin Barr

978-1-877551-31-4

> 'Conveys the joy and sense of discovery in playing video games'
> *The Sunday Star-Times*

Video games attract devotees of all ages and make more money than the movie industry, yet to many people they remain a mystery. Passionate game player and designer Pippin Barr shares fascinating insights that may entice you to give some games a whirl and provides some tips to take existing players to the next level.